101 Ways to Leave the Law

101 Ways to Leave the Law

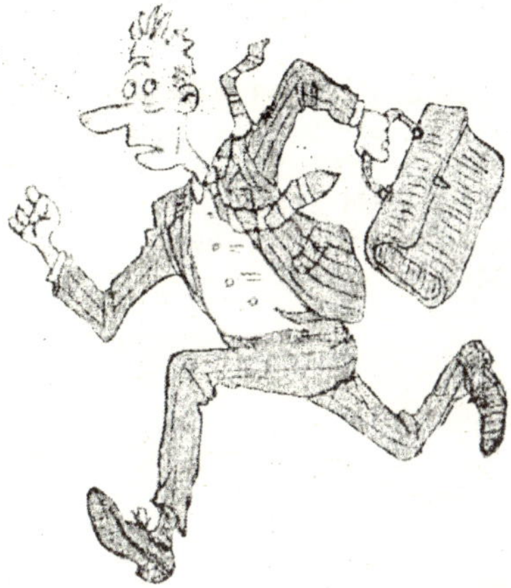

Alex Steuart Williams

FIRST INDIAN REPRINT 2010

Universal
Law Publishing Co. Pvt. Ltd.
NEW DELHI - INDIA

First published in Great Britain in 2009

First Indian Reprint 2010

Published by
UNIVERSAL LAW PUBLISHING CO. PVT. LTD.
C-FF-1A, Dilkhush Industrial Estate (Near Azadpur Metro Station)
G.T. Karnal Road, Delhi-110 033
Tel.: 011- 42381334, 27215334, 27438103, Fax : 011-27458529
E-mail *(For sales inquiries)* : sales@unilawbooks.com
Website : www.unilawbooks.com

Under special arrangement with
J R BOOKS, LONDON (UK)

Licensed for Sale in Indian Sub-Continent

ISBN 978-81-7534-965-0

A catalogue record for this book is available from the British Library.

Printed and bound in India at Glorious Printers, New Delhi

For Sarah,
who really, honestly, doesn't
want to leave the law

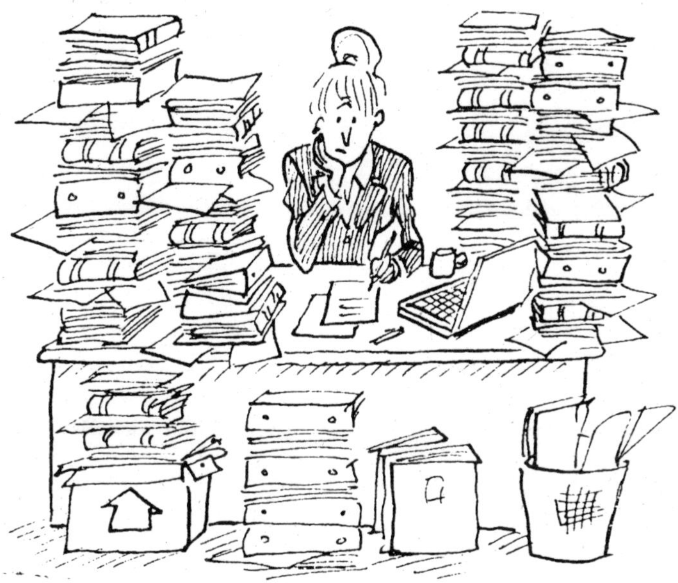

Introduction

The author John Grisham was once asked, 'In your years as a lawyer, what was the most satisfying thing about the law?' to which he replied simply: 'Getting out of it.' It's a typical lawyer's answer and it captures the dark humour with which many of us regard our own profession. Highly motivated, intelligent people poring over sub-clauses and skeleton arguments wishing they were any place but there. A beach perhaps, or the top of a mountain, or tending their garden, or kicking back watching the cricket on a lazy Sunday afternoon. Anywhere but the hothouse which is the law. Where time is a commodity and justice seems like the preserve of fiction.

Or that's how they'd have you believe it if you heard them in the bar after a few drinks. Yet they rarely leave – or even come close to leaving – blaming the mortgage or the school fees and the like. Perhaps the reality is that, despite it all, most lawyers like being lawyers. It might be the money, or the sense of belonging to a recognised profession or institution. It might be the thrill of the chase. Getting the bit between your teeth and fighting your corner on behalf of the client. Or it might even be trying to do some good in the world. I mean, hey, let's not push the boat out and all, but just maybe.

All of which has been wonderfully captured in this book. The daydreams of telling the boss exactly what you think and throwing all the years of hard work down the drain in a moment of liberating honesty. The fantasy of truly chucking it all in and going out and doing something less boring instead. In this book, anything goes. There are no restrictions and the liberated lawyer is given free rein. The imagination can run wild and the result is a hilarious collection of cartoons which encapsulates the ultimate fantasy not only of many lawyers but of anyone who has ever worked in an office. It is a privilege to introduce this book.

Tim Kevan, 22 July 2009

Type the email you *really* want to send to your client

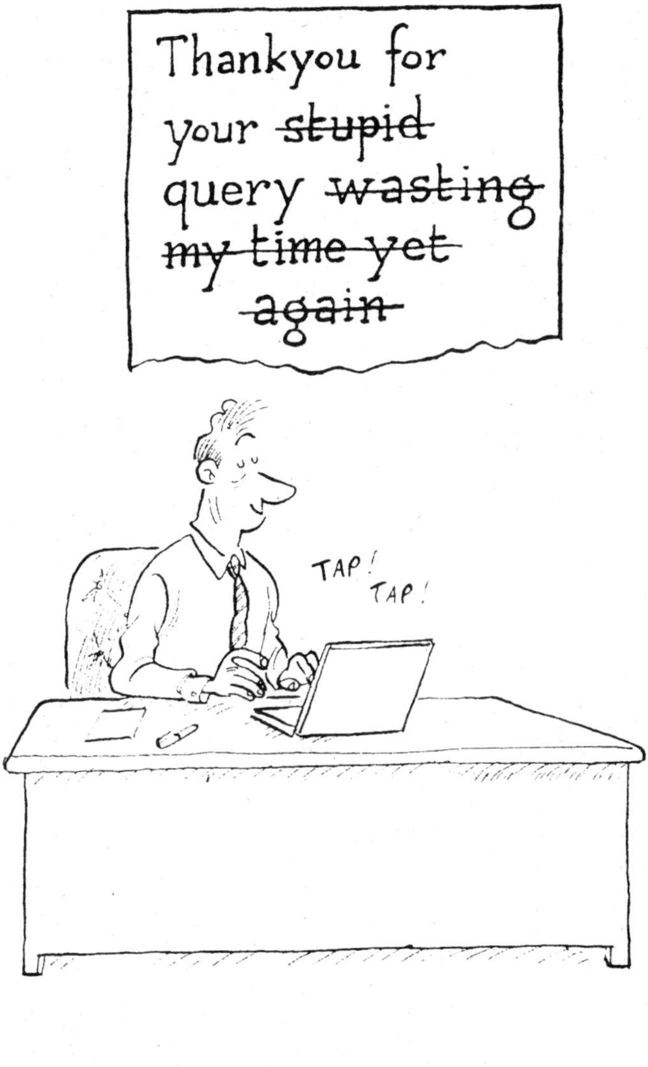

Tell the truth on your time sheets (booked flight, called Mum, long lunch)

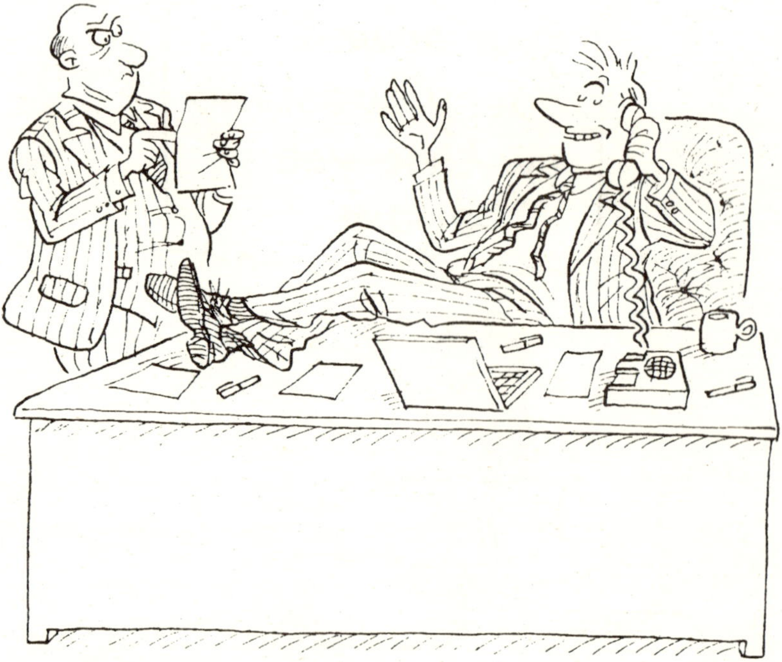

Learn to play guitar

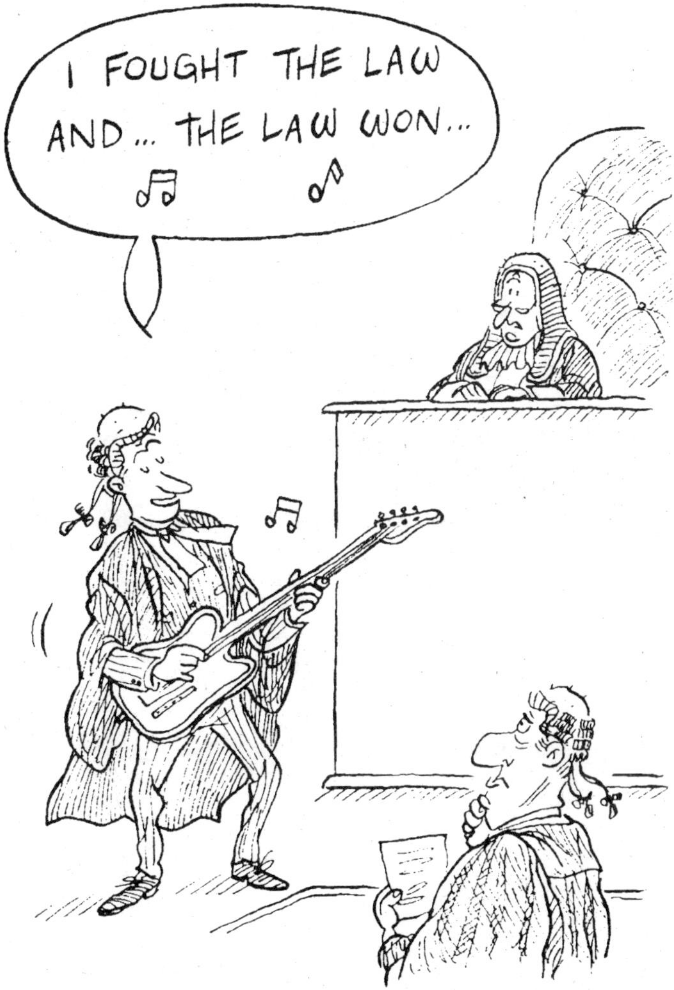

Give the other side the documents they asked for and are actually entitled to

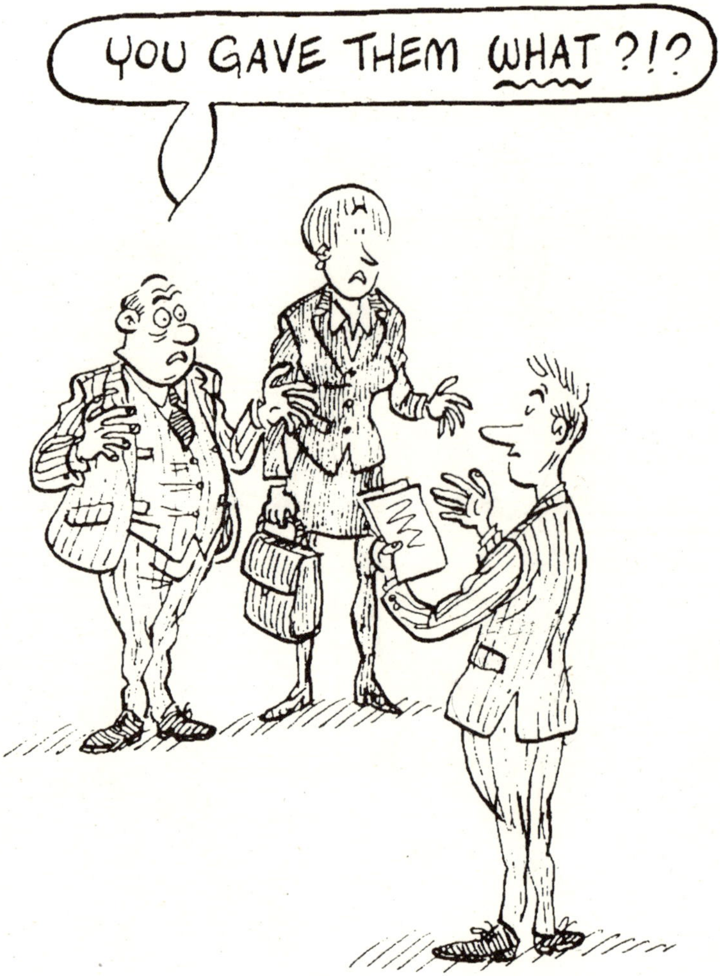

If your client complains about the bill, give him the senior partner's home phone number and suggest that he call any time between midnight and 7am

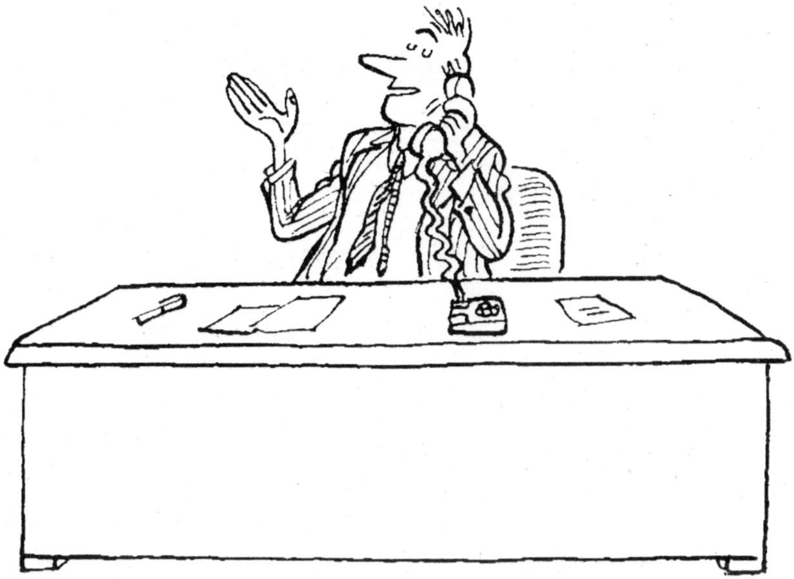

Find religion

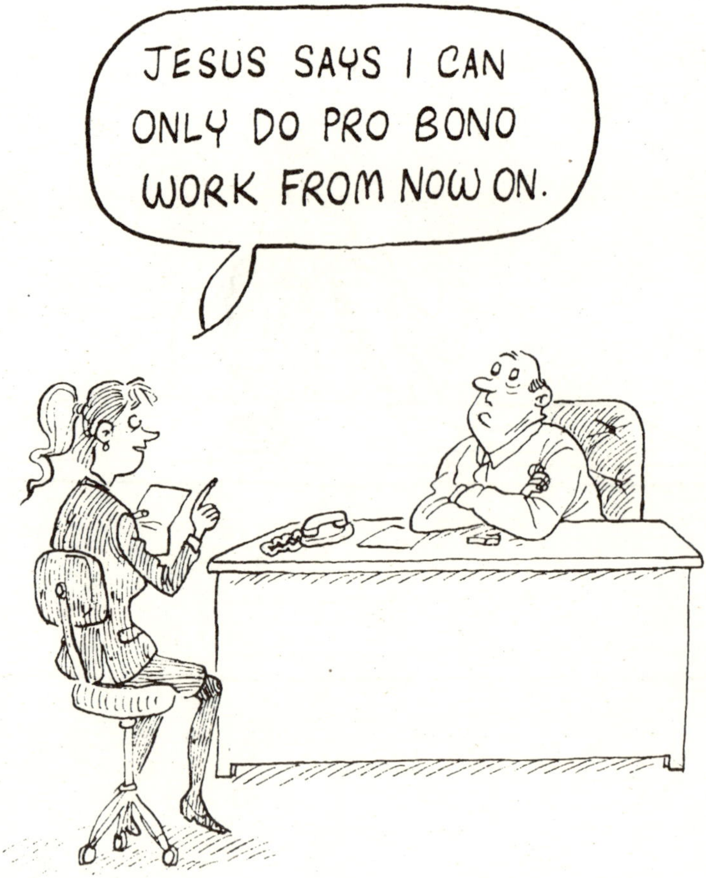

Explain to the government that what they want to do is against the law

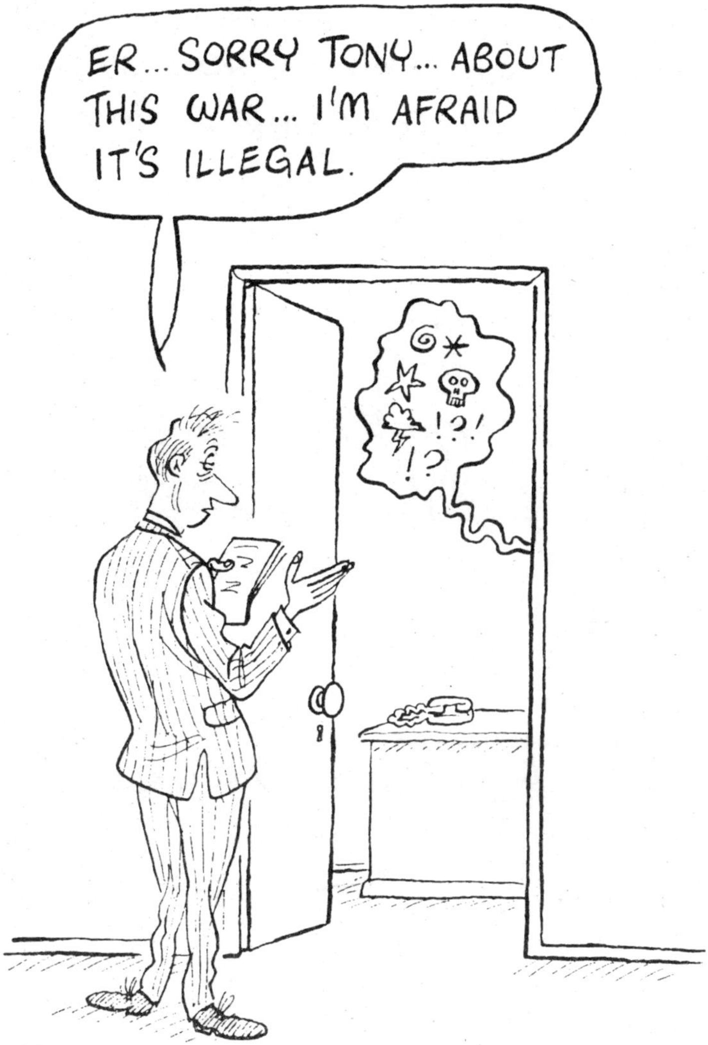

Get out early

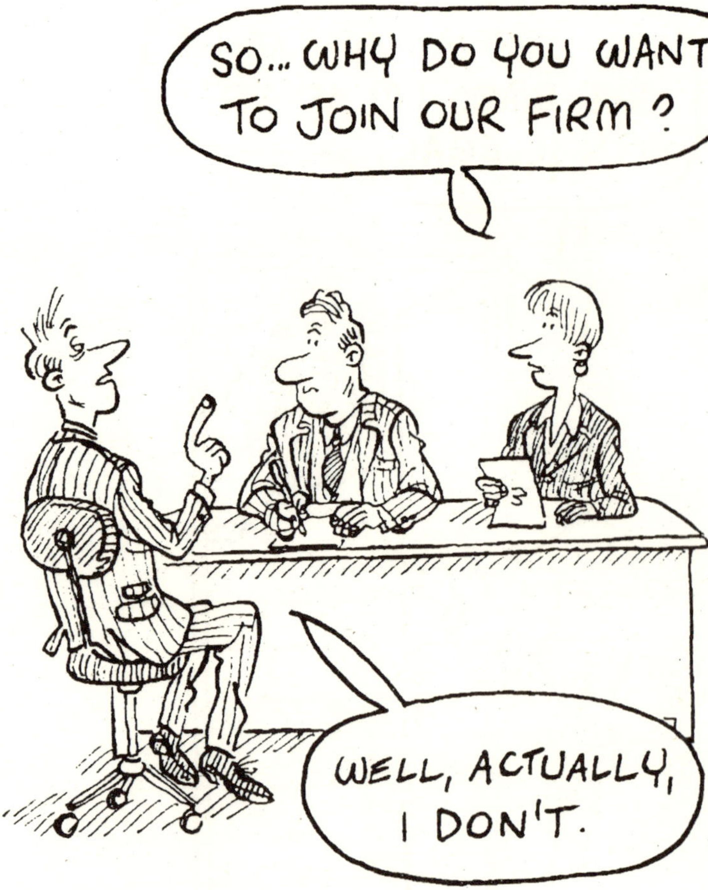

Install a taxi meter on your desk so your client can see exactly how much every minute is costing him

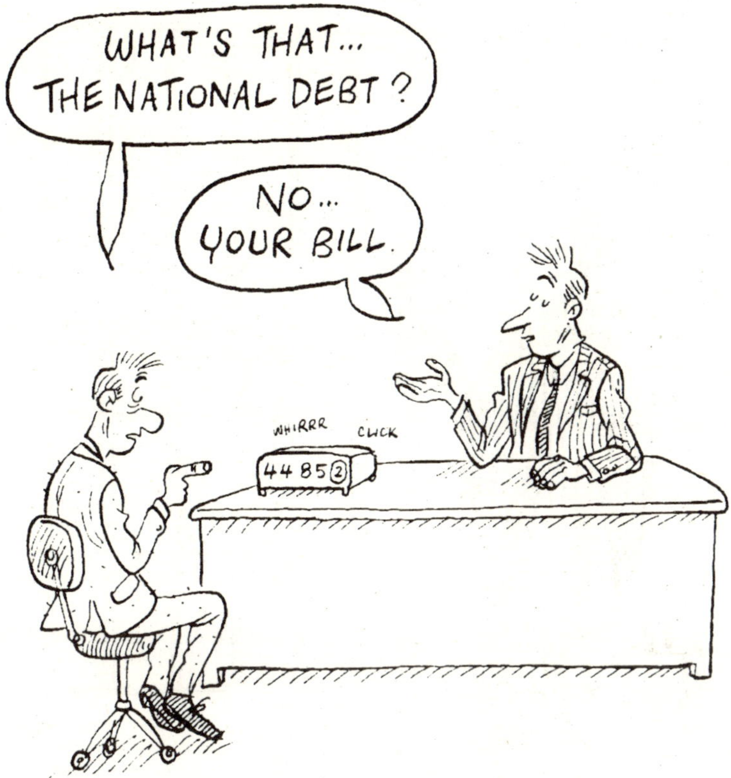

Tell your client to stop stealing for a living (which he obviously isn't any good at), and get a proper job

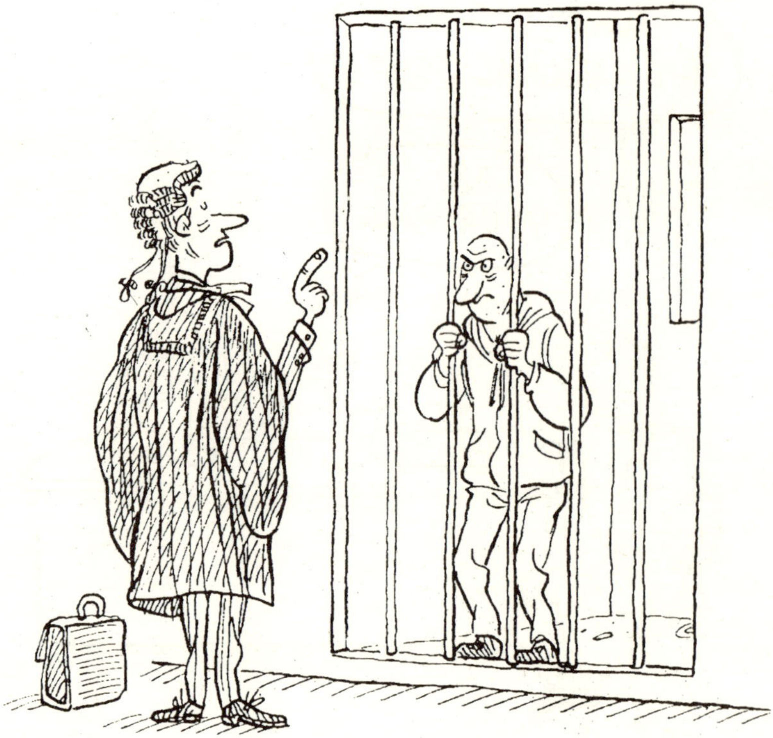

Bill the hours you actually spent working on the case

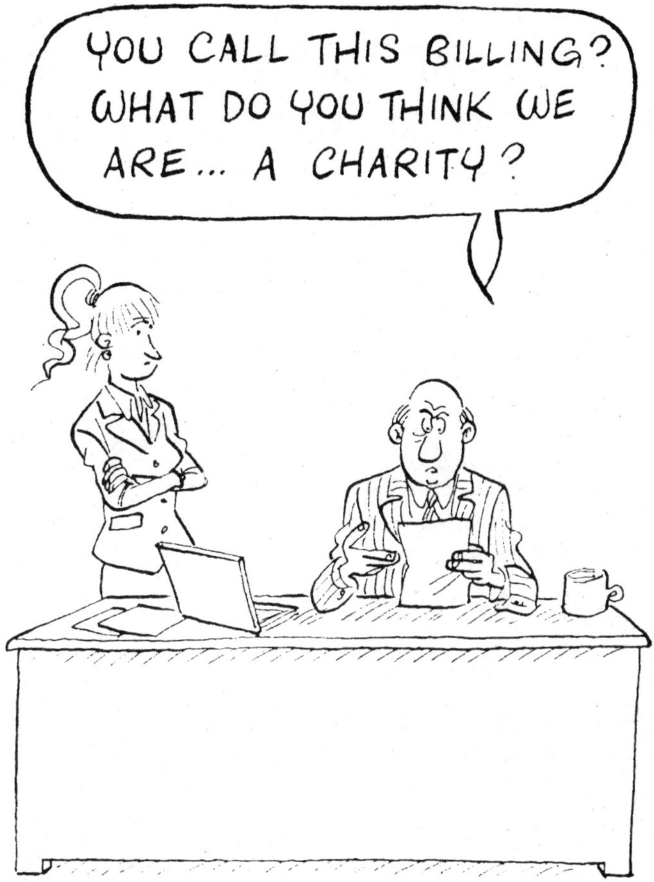

Get that boob job you've always wanted

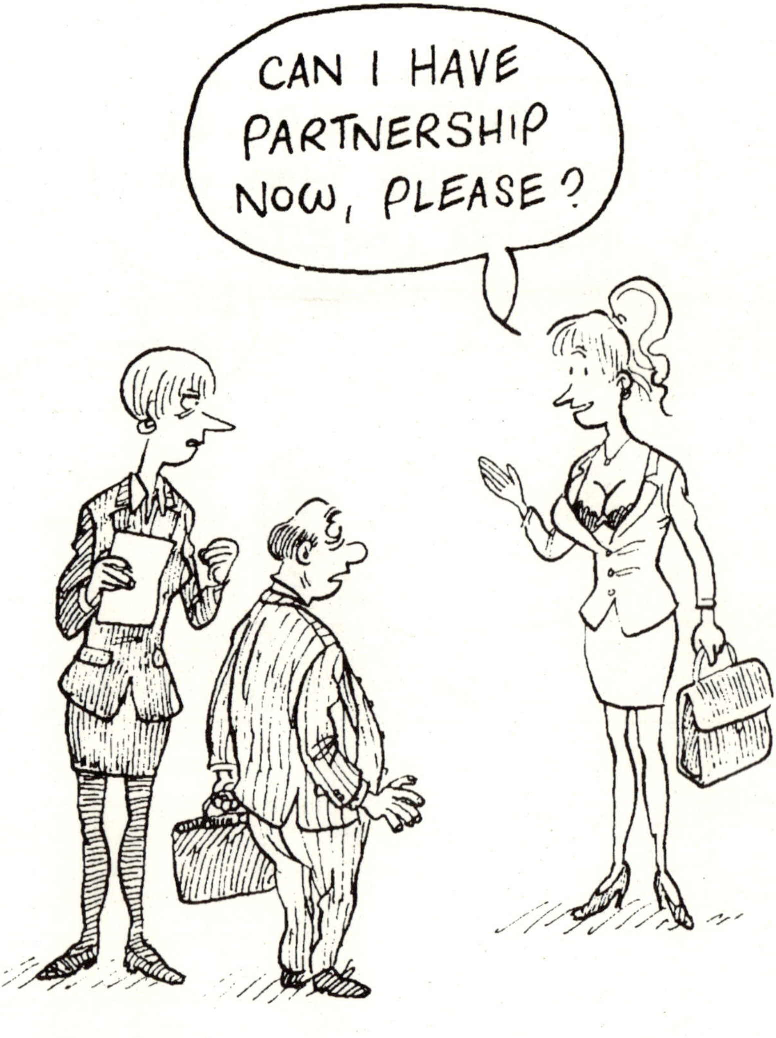

Suggest to your client that he purchase several bars of gold and drop them in the Thames, rather than embark on pointless and costly litigation

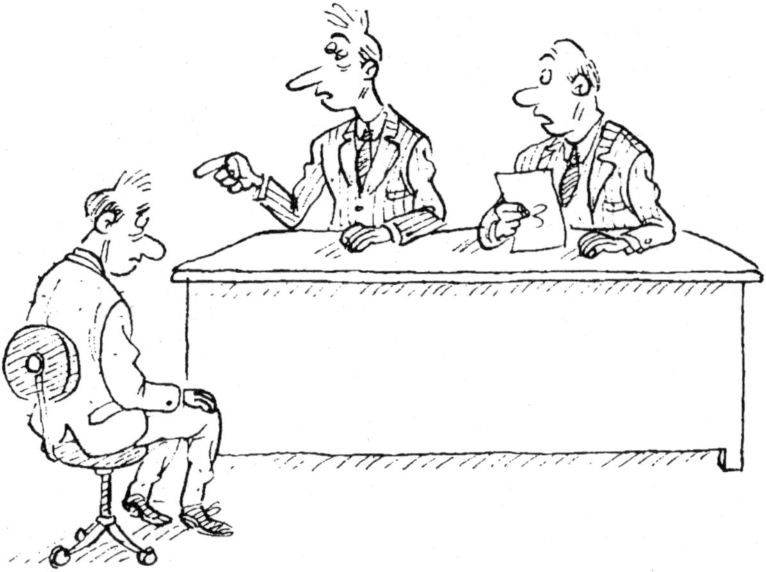

When asked to do some 'blue sky thinking', do just that

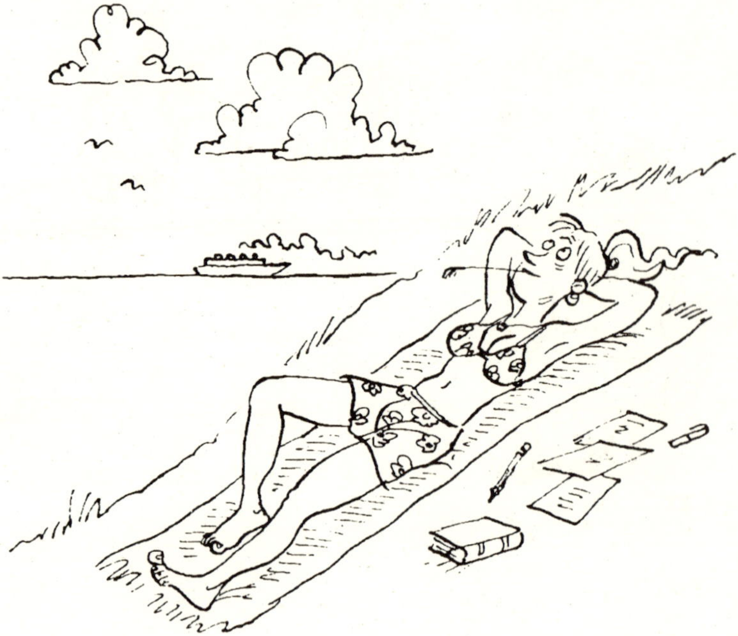

Take *habeus corpus* literally

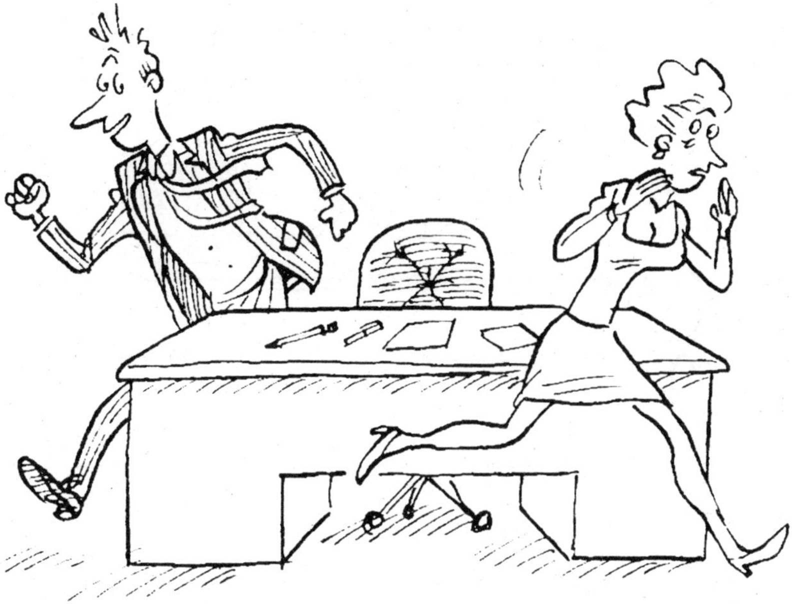

Be honest with your client about his chances

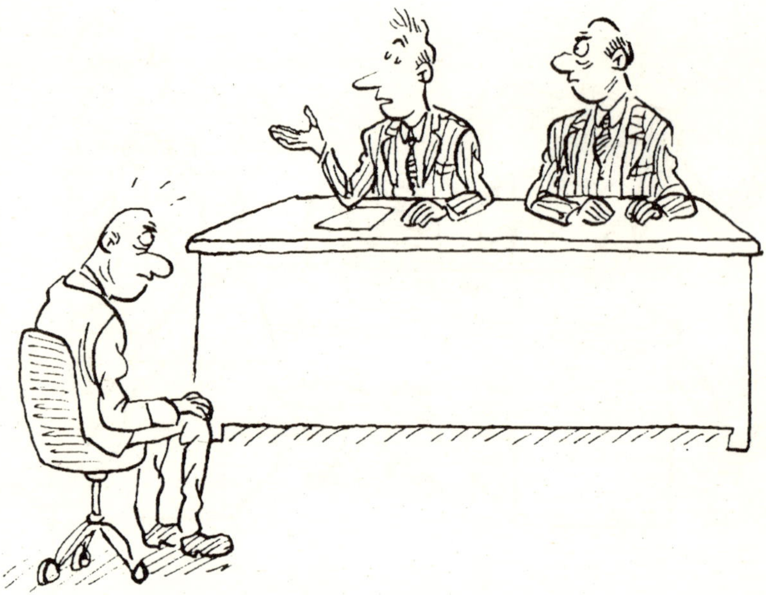

Bake a BlackBerry® pie

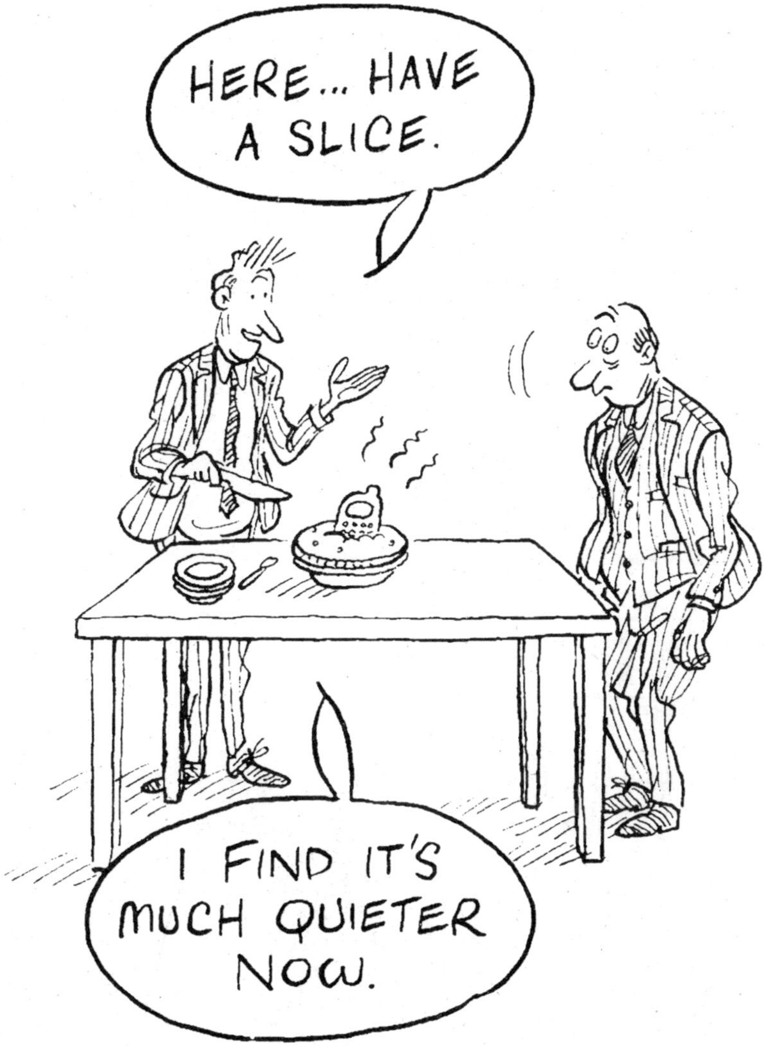

Hand the judge a brown envelope stuffed with cash

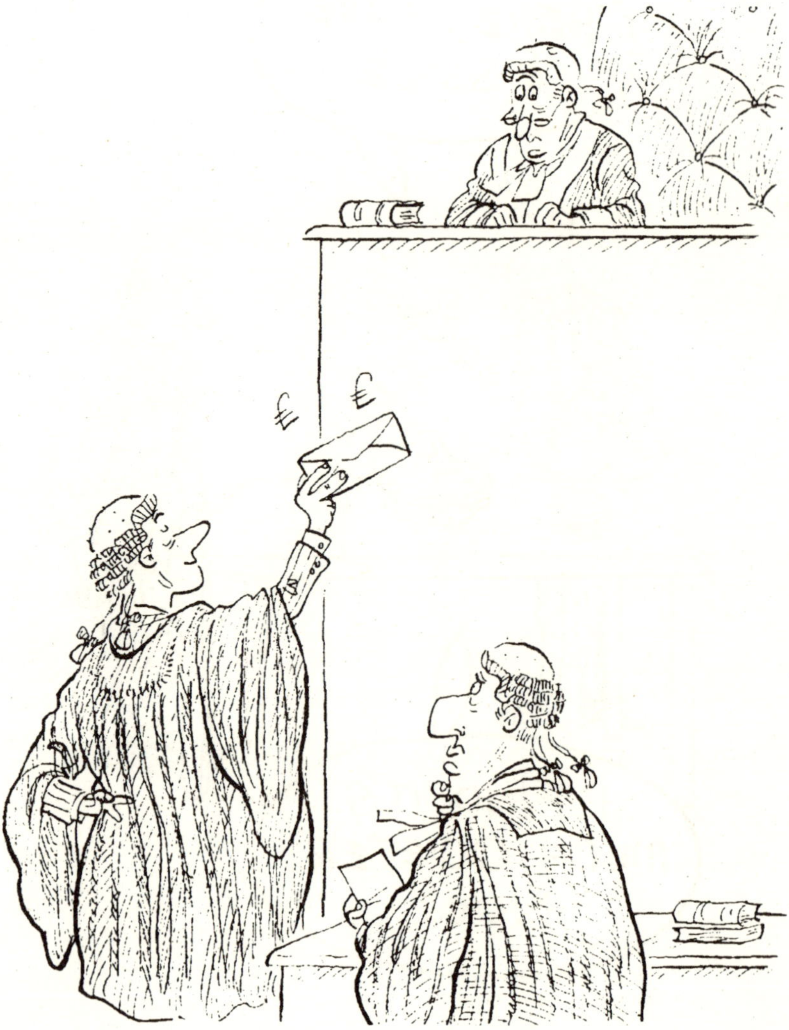

Photocopy your bottom at the Christmas party
and email it to the firm's client list

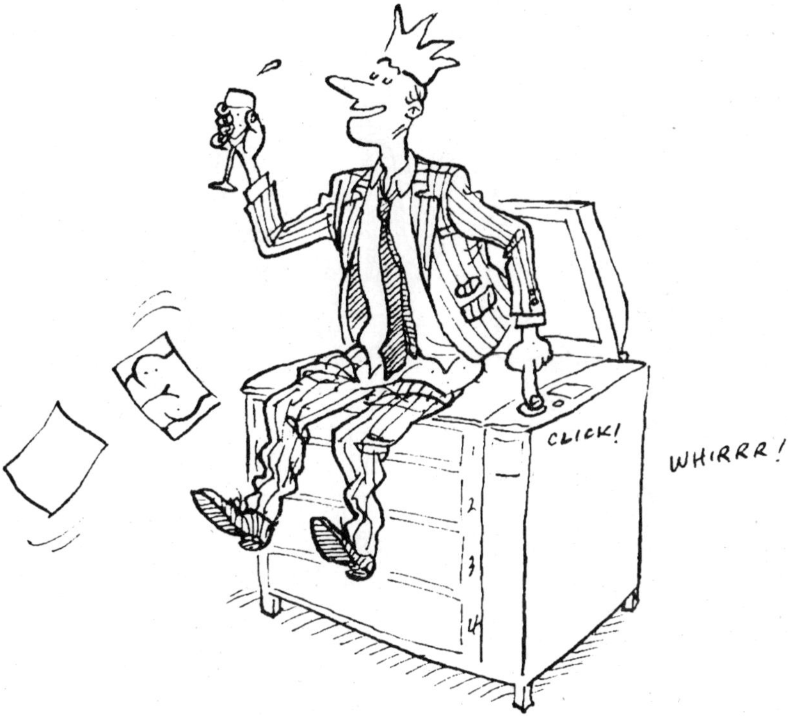

Tell the press that your client is as guilty as sin
and the jury should never have let him off

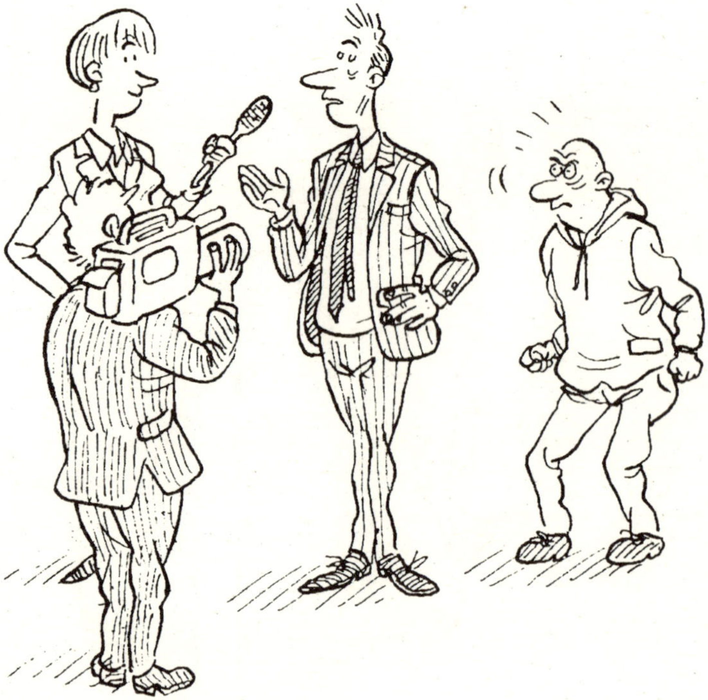

Dress casual on casual Fridays

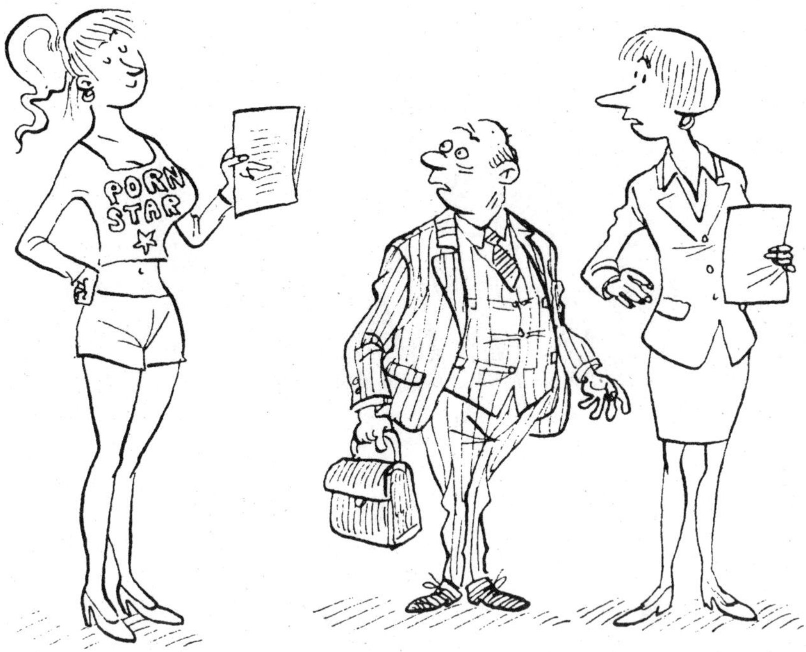

Think that law is about justice

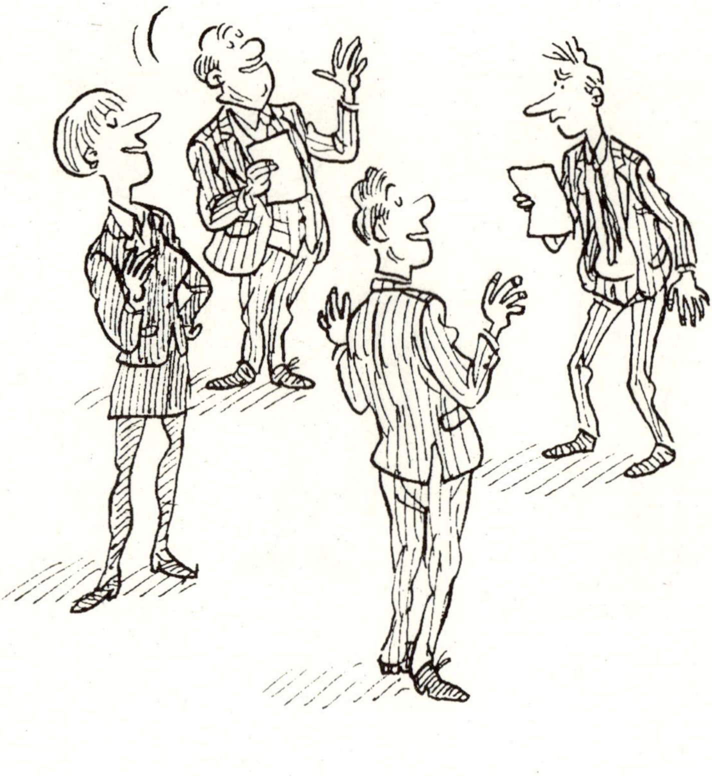

Give the judge a coin and suggest that he flip it, because it's just as likely to do justice as he is

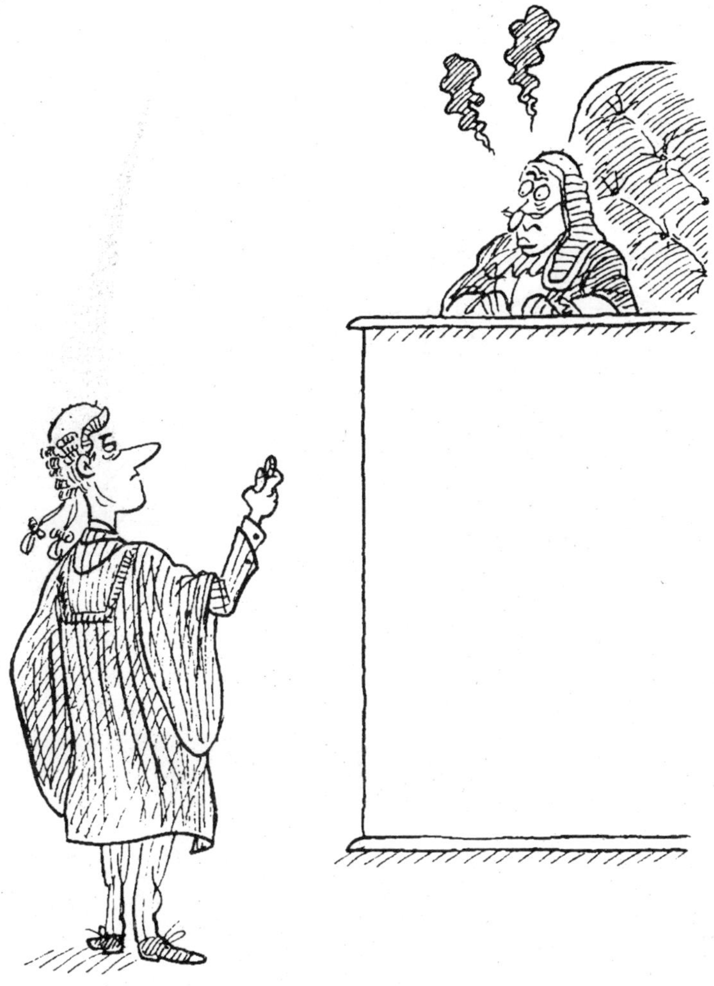

Fly to the Cayman Islands with the contents of the client bank account, and never come back

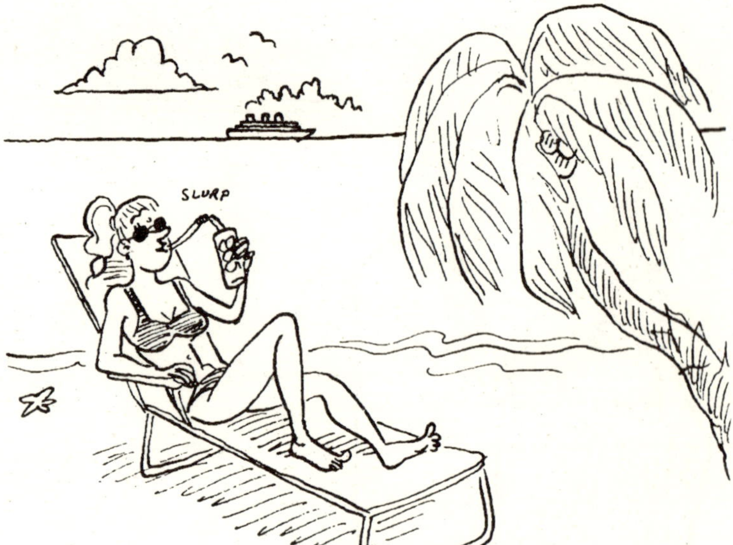

Explain to the press that diversity at your firm means that some partners went to Oxford, and others to Cambridge

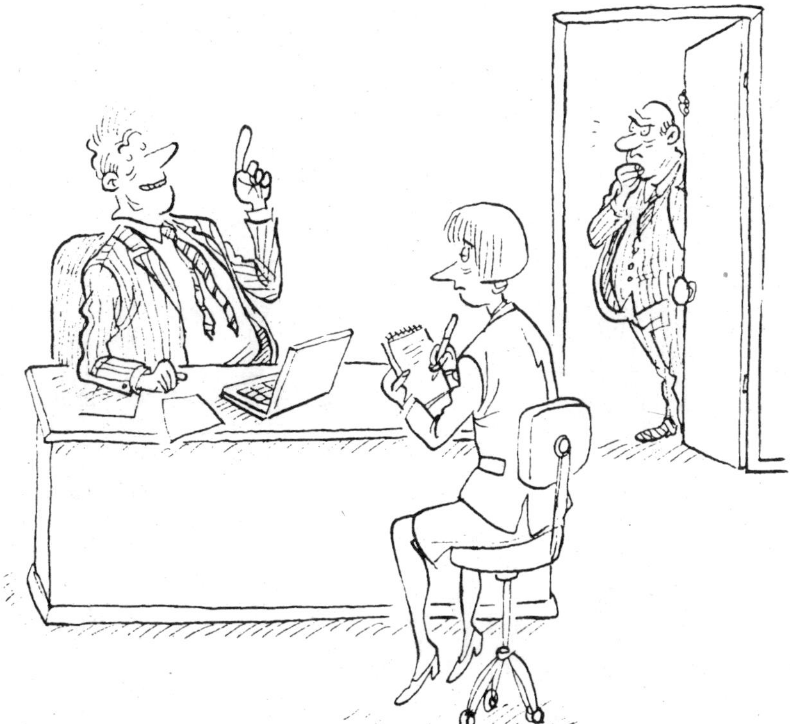

Bring your dog to work

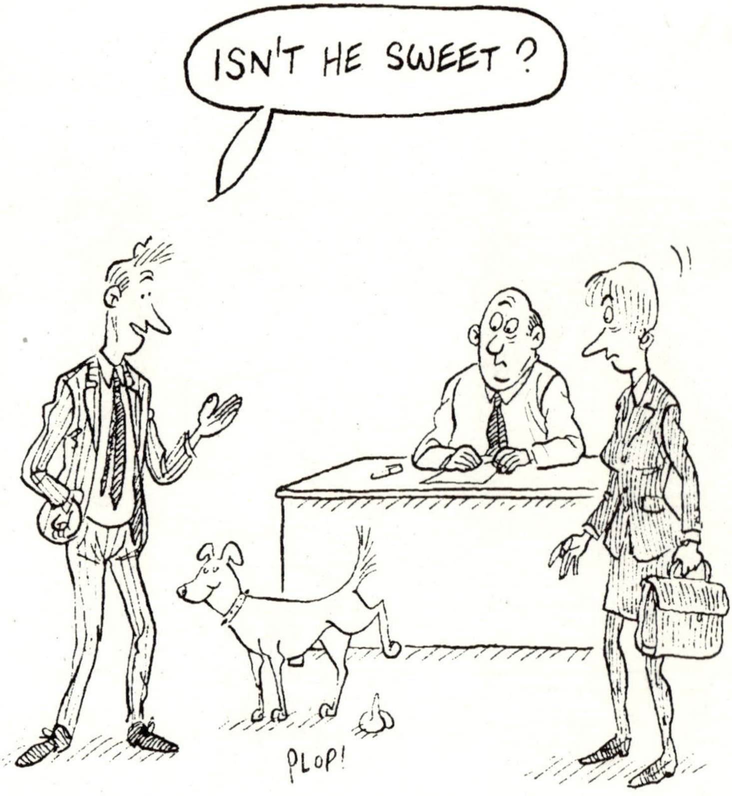

Hand out leaflets offering a 50 per cent discount on the firm's fees

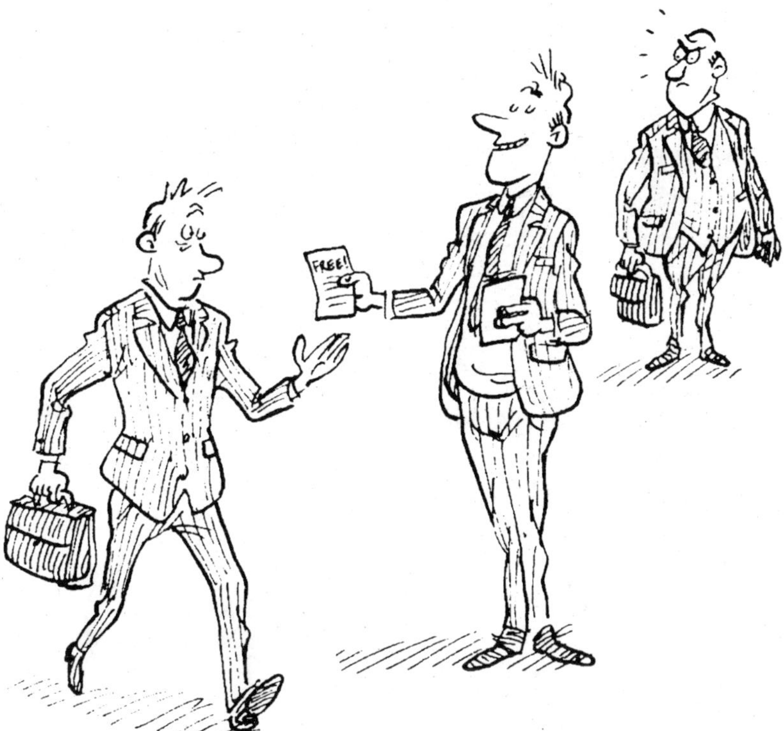

After a conference call, tell your colleagues just how stupid your client is, without realising you haven't hung up the phone properly

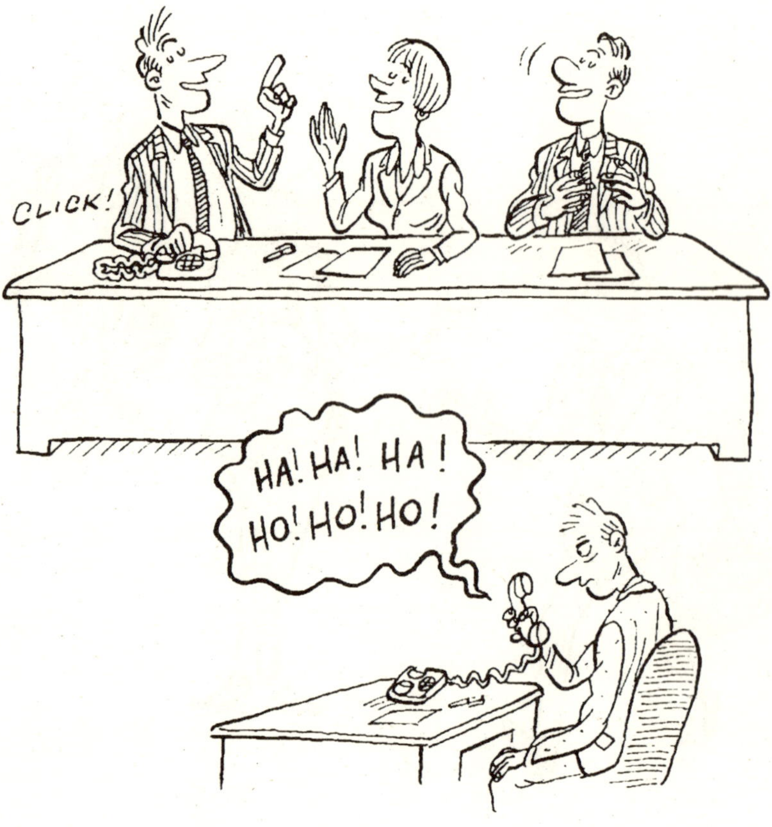

Doze off during the senior partner's speech at the firm's annual dinner

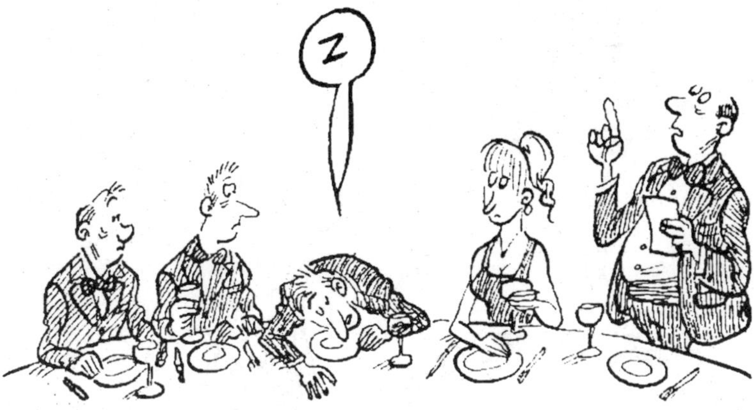

Turn down a client function, explaining that you would rather be burned alive than go bowling with a third tier insurance company

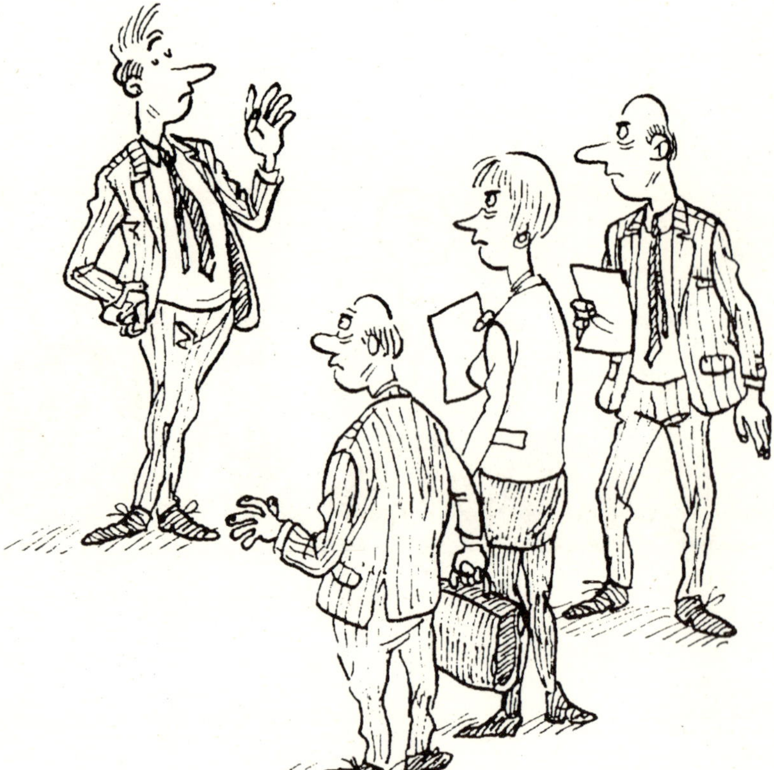

Print out some porn from the shared office printer . . . and then forget you did

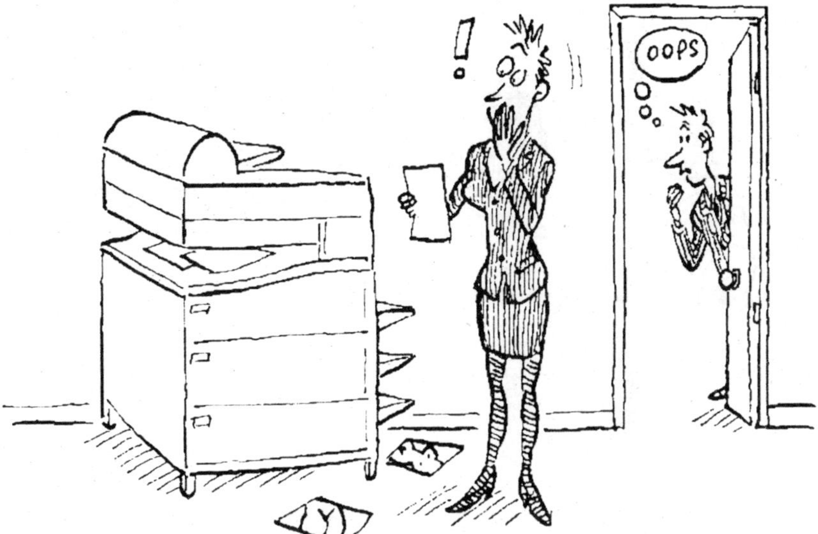

Explain to your colleagues in front of the client how, if they really wanted to help him, they could all cut their fees by 20 per cent

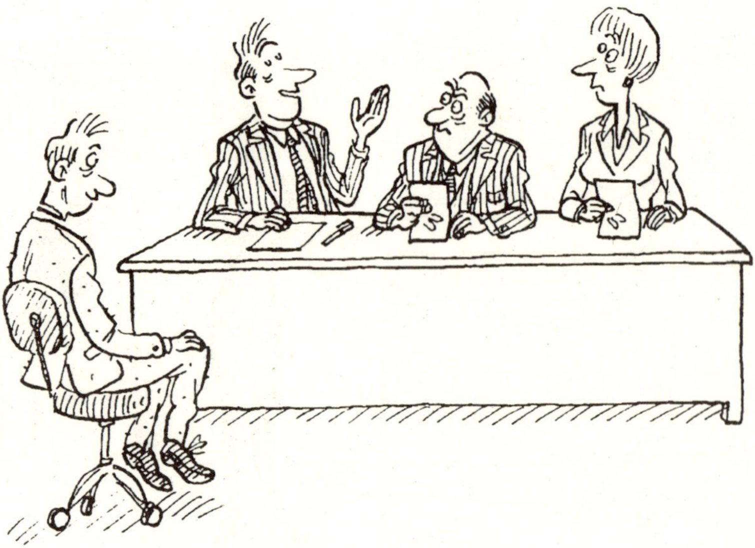

Draft a document in plain English that your client could actually read and understand

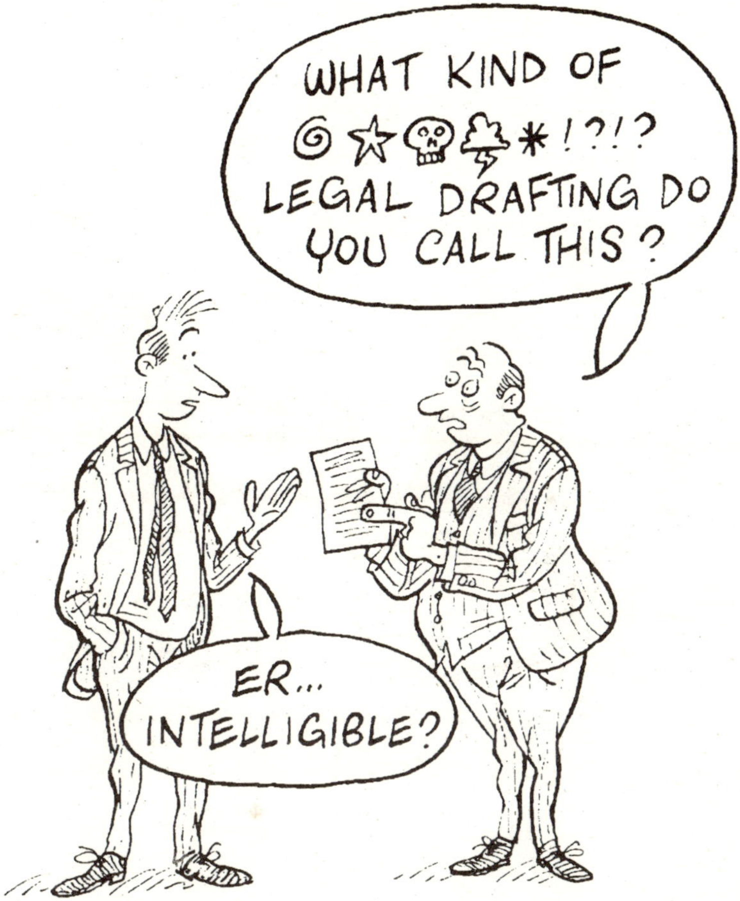

When told by the senior partner that he welcomes independent thought and criticism, offer some

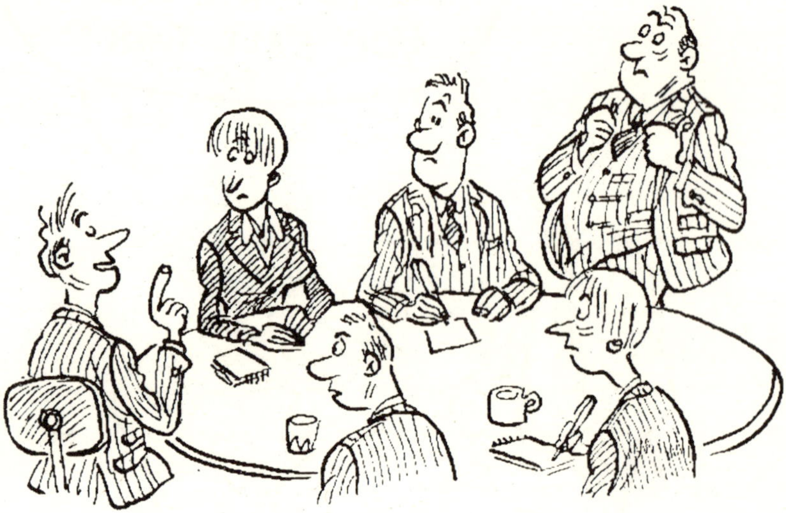

Don't wash for two weeks

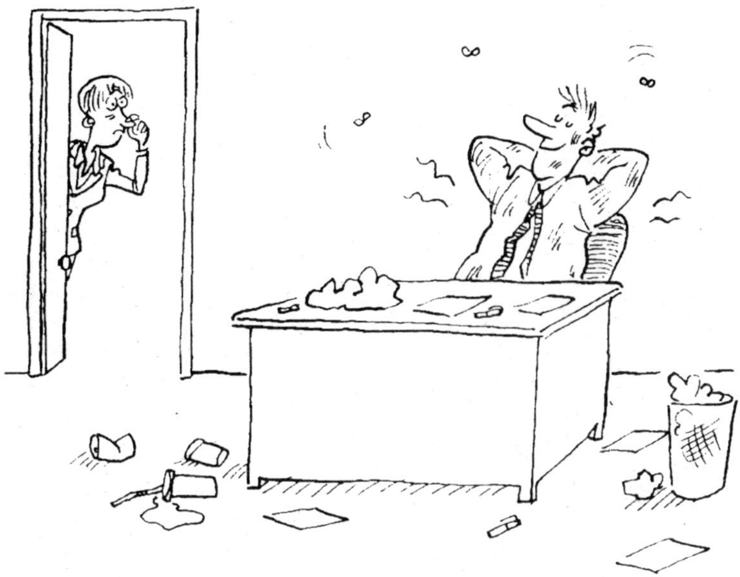

Eat the office canteen food

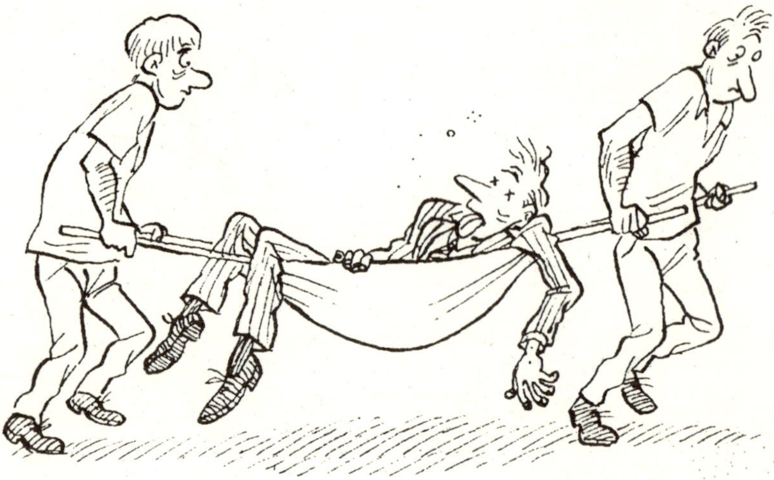

Drop the partner in it at a client conference

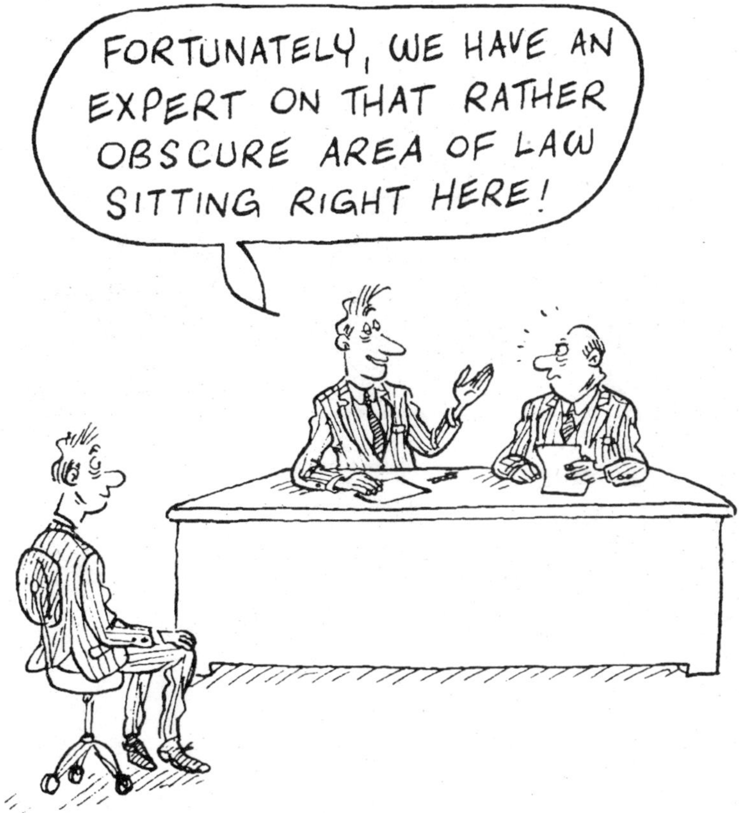

Suggest that the firm's annual partnership meeting should be held in Eastbourne, rather than the Caribbean, to improve the firm's carbon footprint

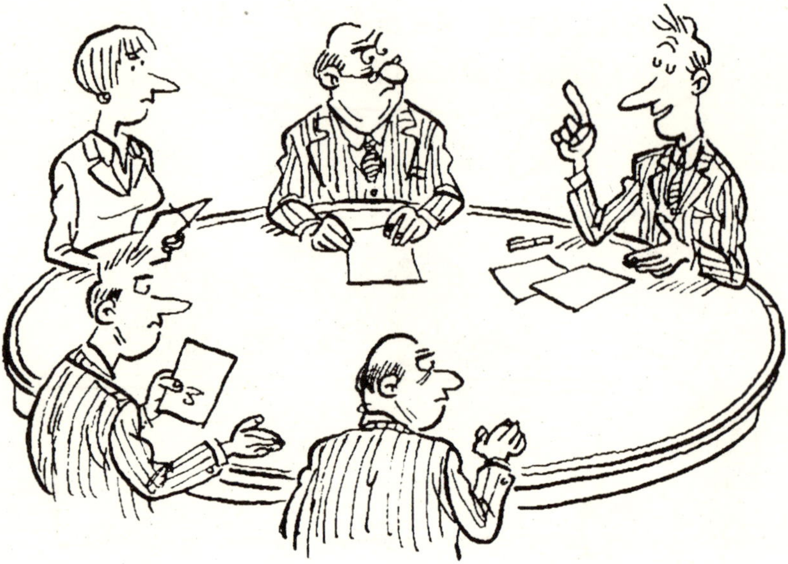

Fake a heart attack in court

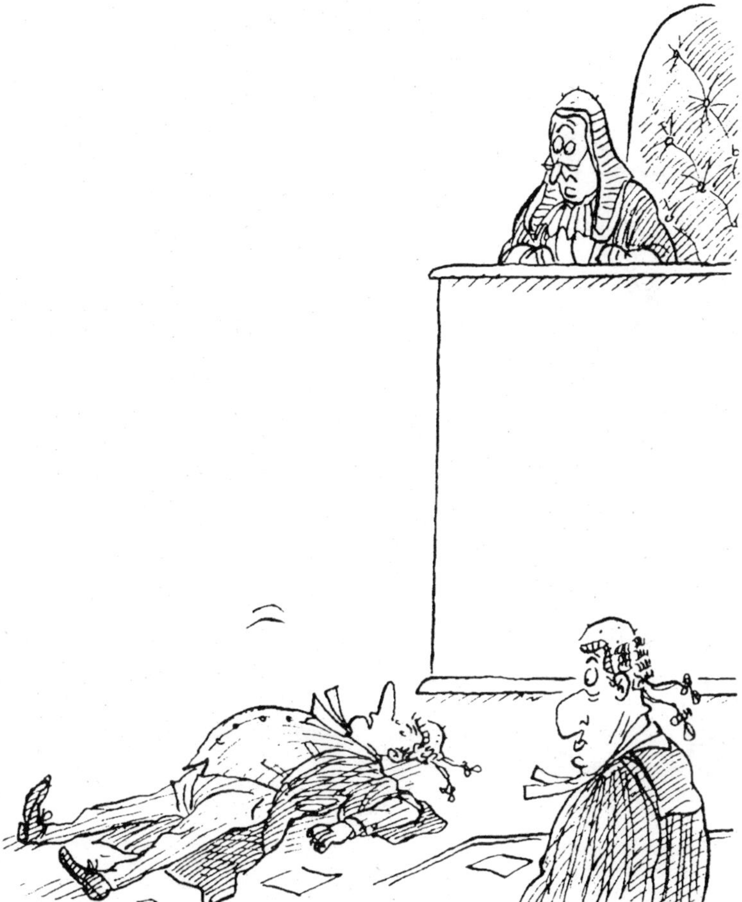

Practice criminal law

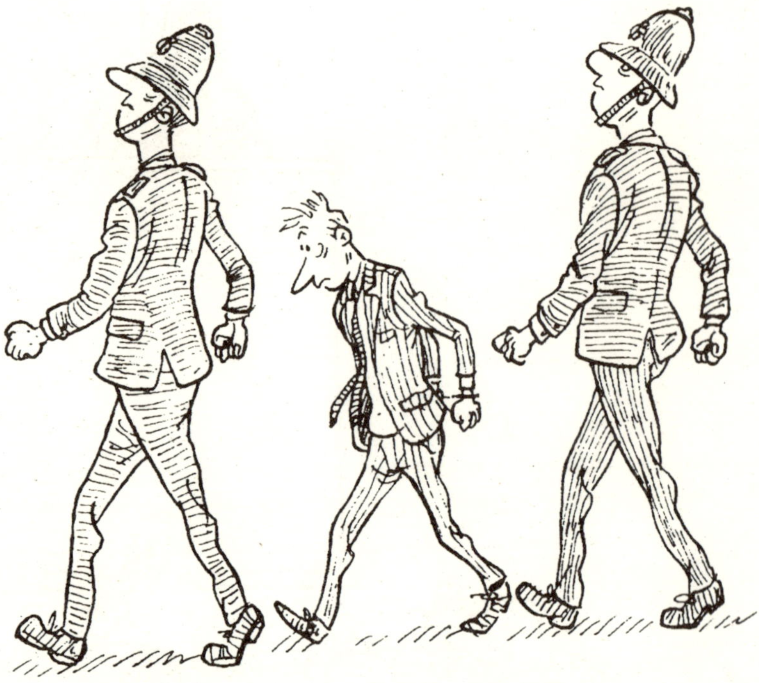

Have a bash at advising on foreign law

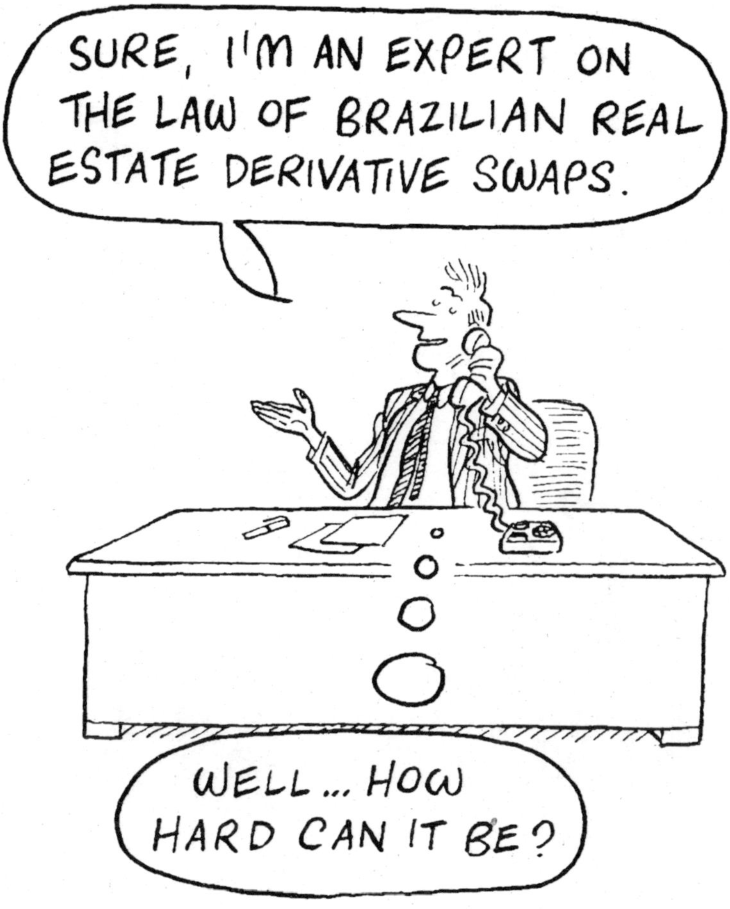

Pretend you're in an episode of *LA Law*

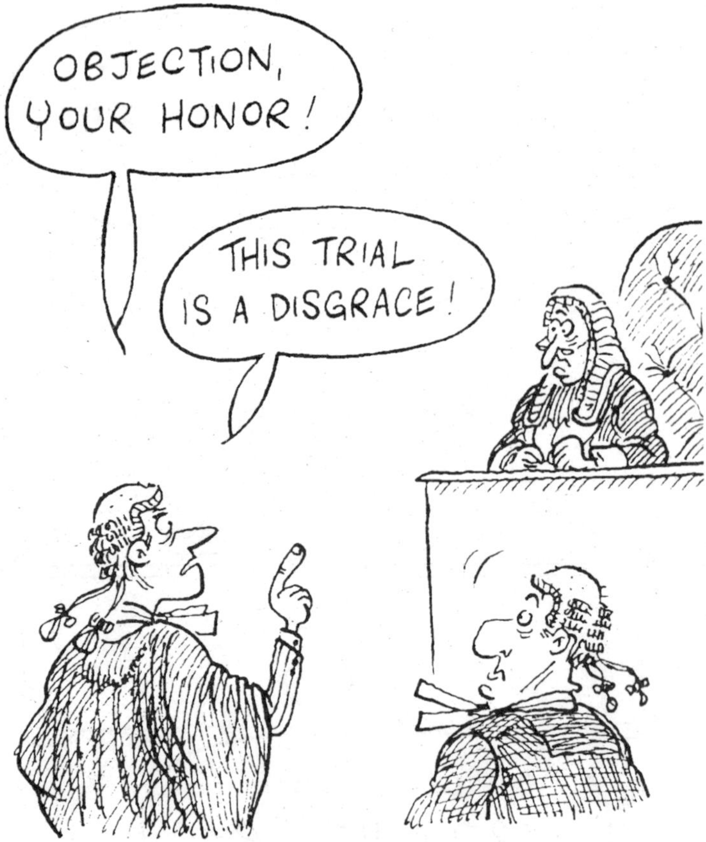

Fail to realise that a contract of employment which specifies you will work '9.30am to 5.30pm . . . and other such hours as the firm may from time to time require', means that the firm owns your soul 24/7

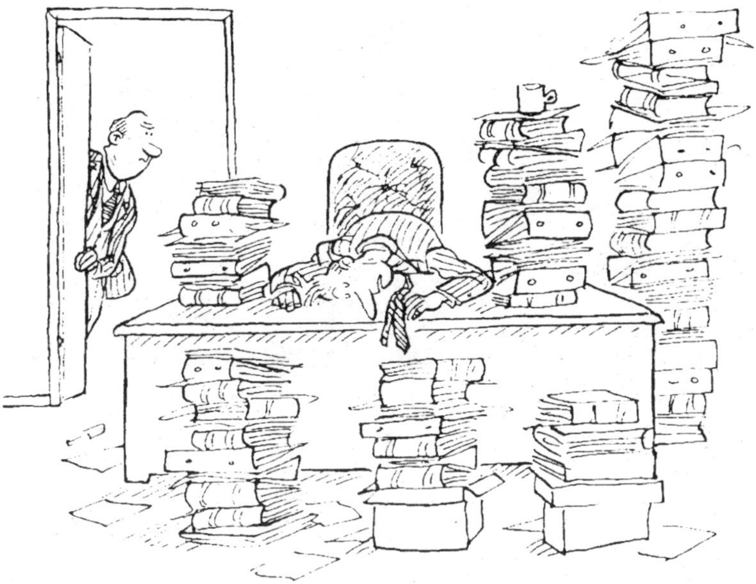

Take 'eat what you kill' literally

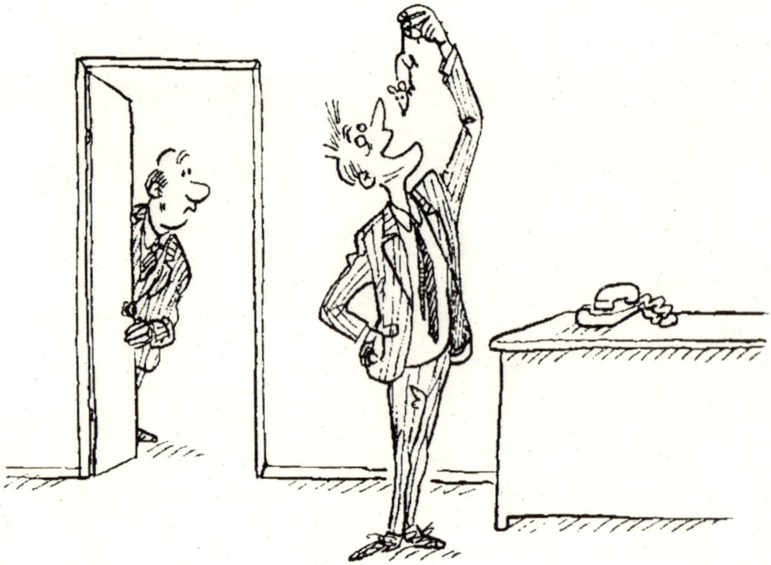

Explain to your client that the purpose of the legal system is to enrich lawyers

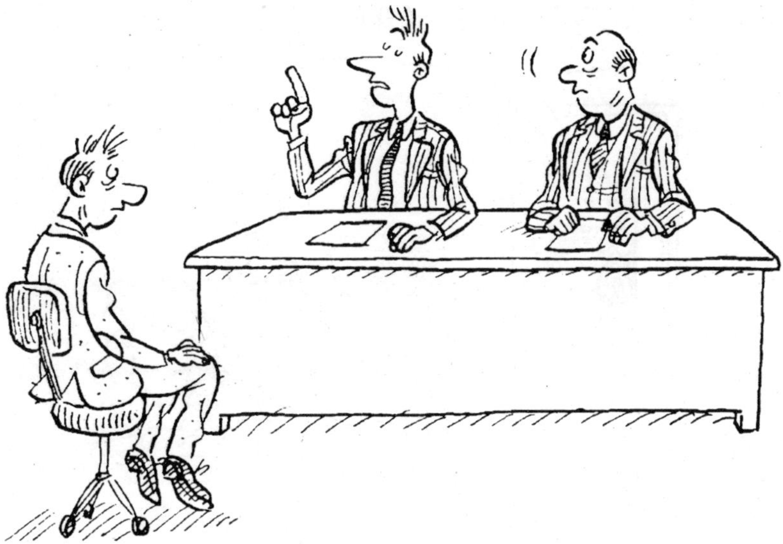

Take the senior partner's 'open door' policy literally

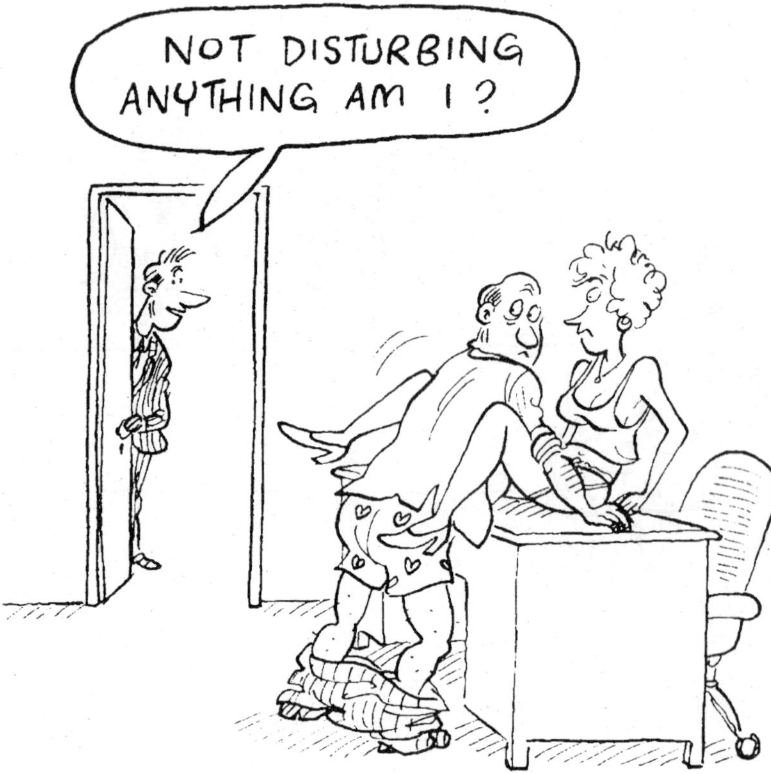

Tell your client the truth

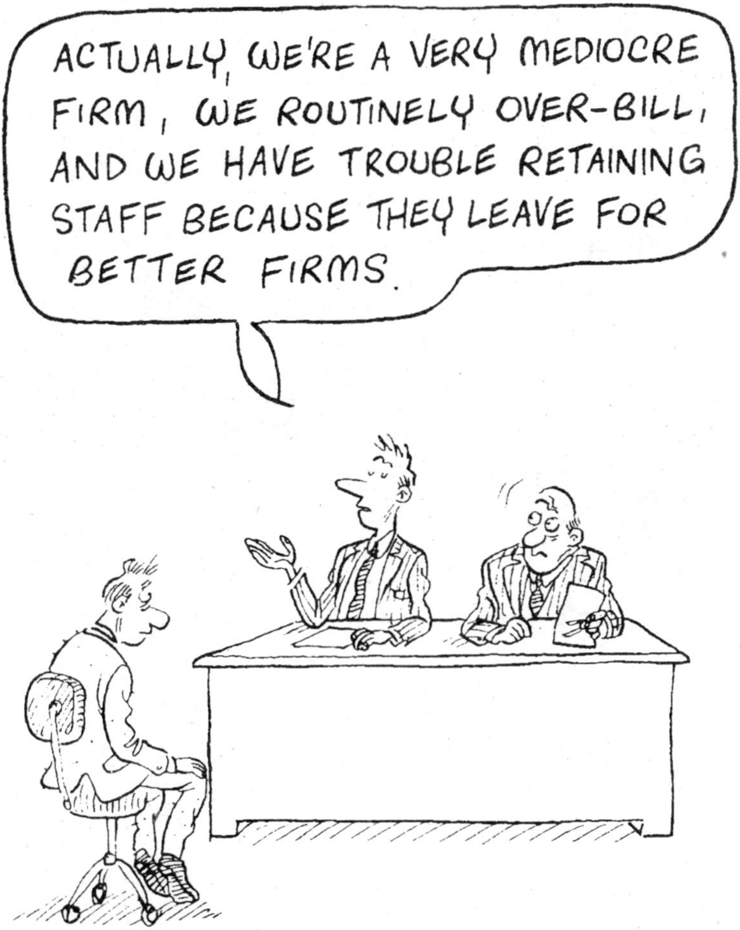

At your interview, tell the firm that the reason you want to join them is that all the good ones turned you down

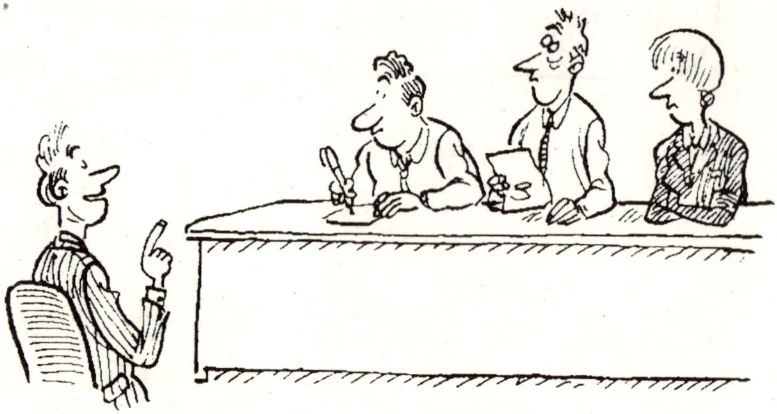

Challenge the senior partner on how he managed to record three billable hours on a witness statement that hasn't even been started yet

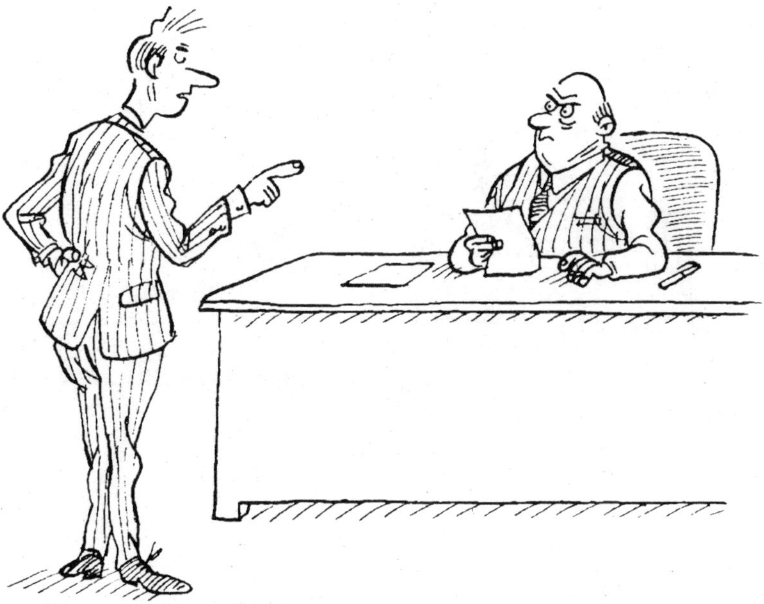

Sleep with the senior partner's wife

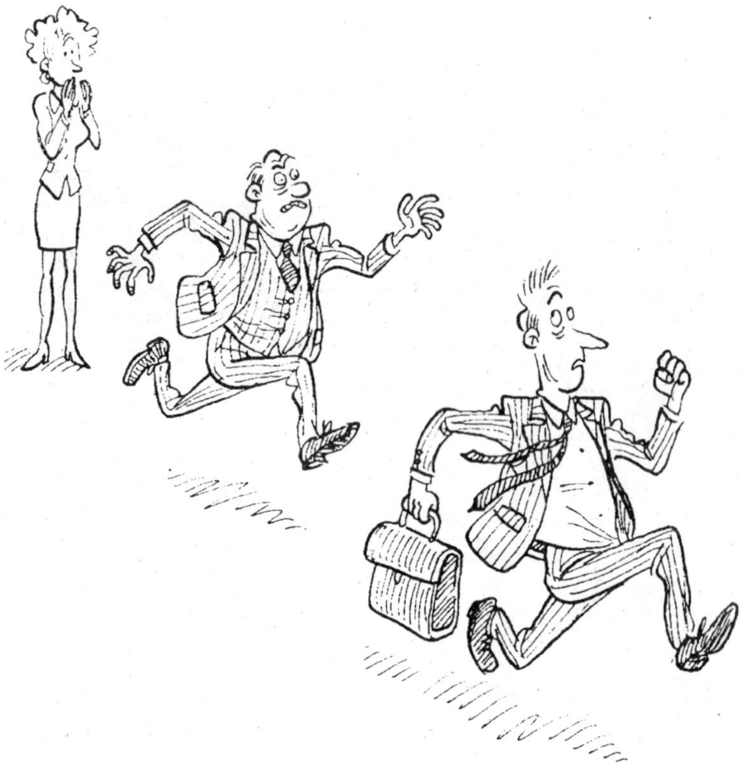

Tell your client not to be so greedy, and to settle his differences like a decent human being

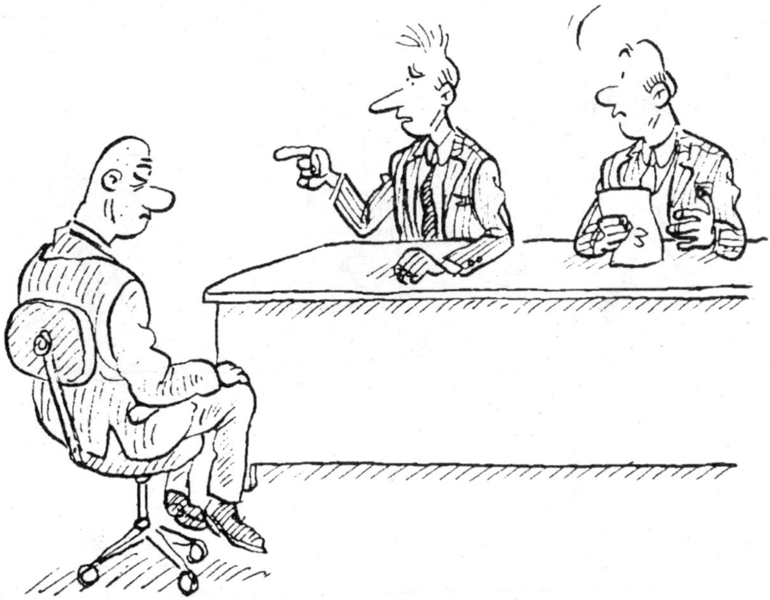

Forget that the golden rule of time sheets is not 'never tell a lie', but 'never get caught'

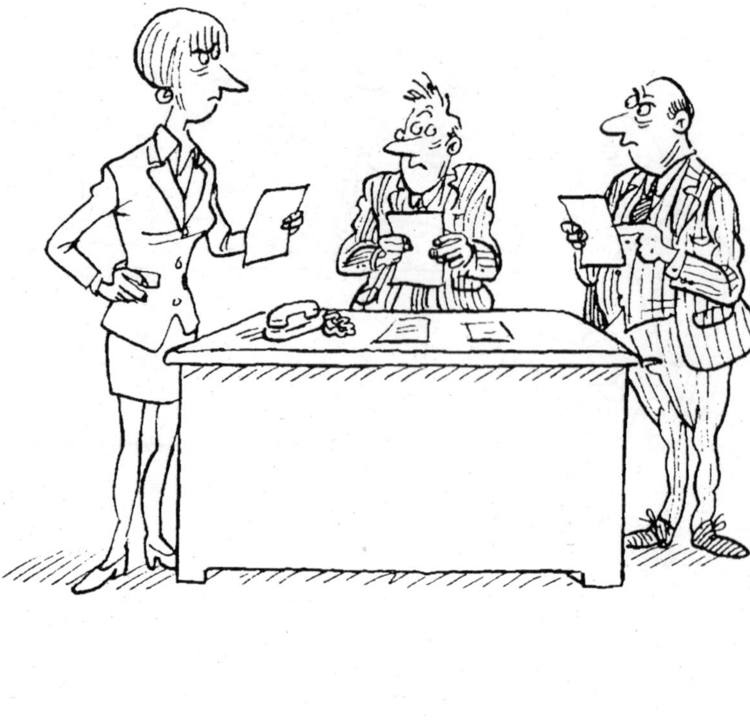

Thrash the firm's wealthiest client at golf

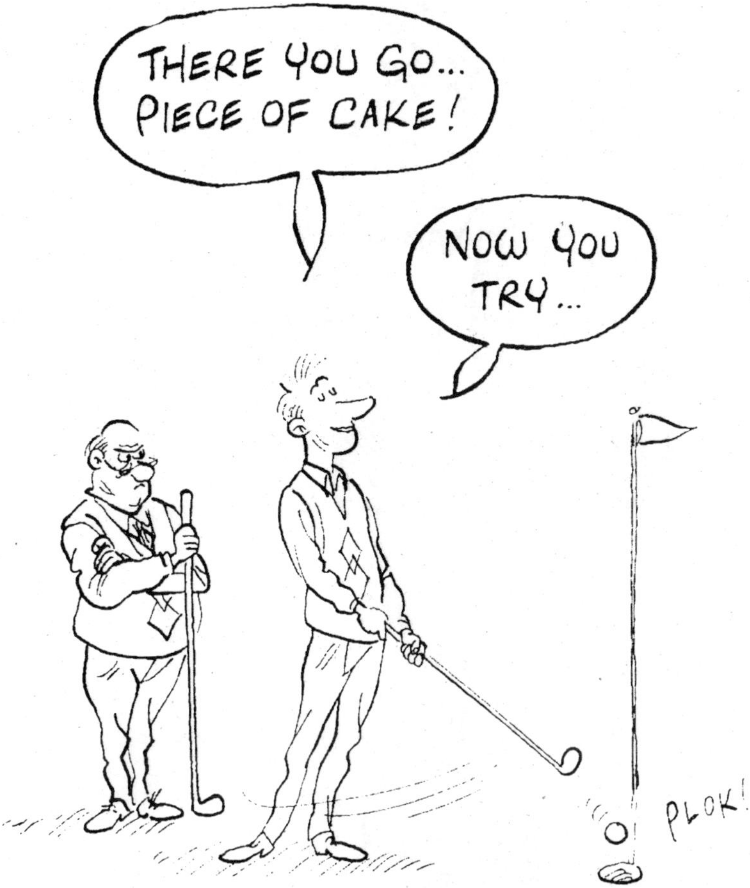

Attempt to commit hara-kiri with the office stapler

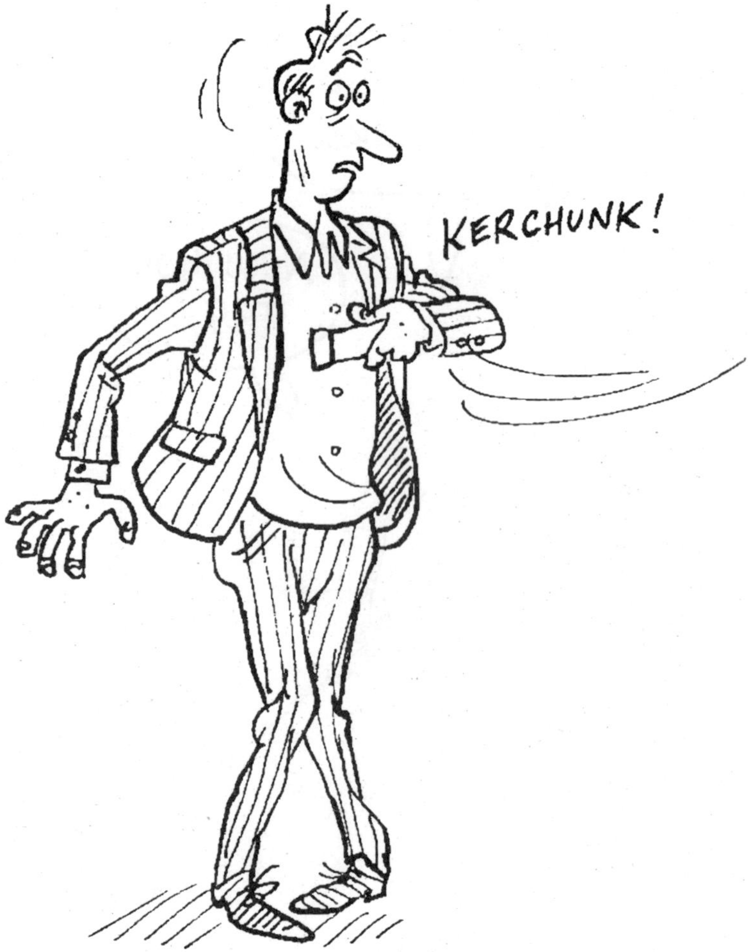

Telephone your biggest client and tell them how much you hate them

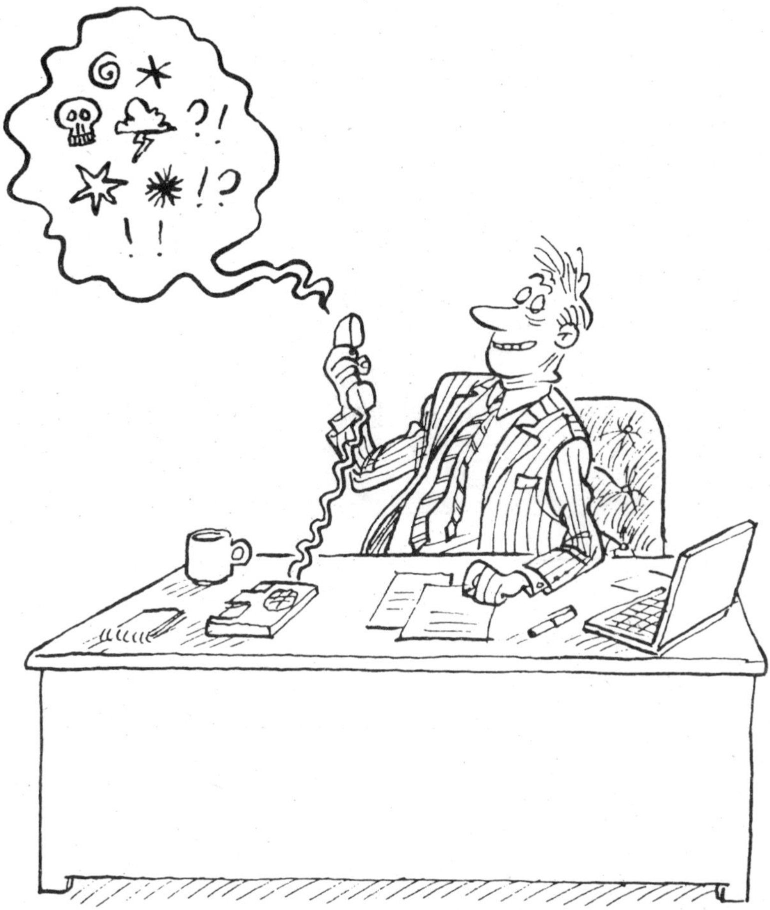

Chair a client meeting after switching to a special diet consisting entirely of dried apricots and baked beans

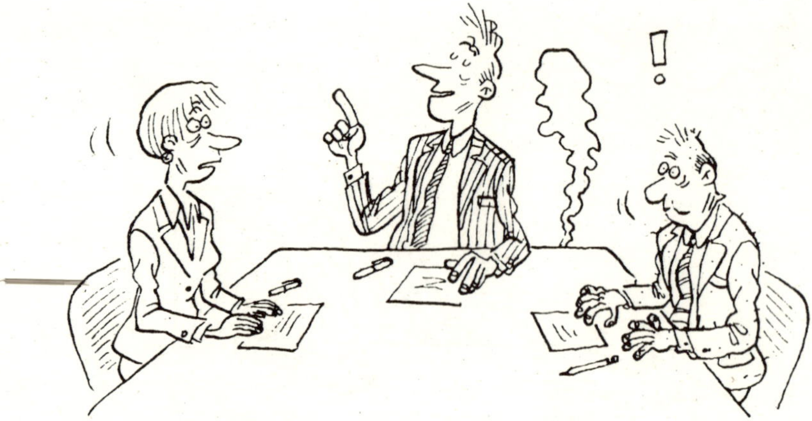

Slip out at lunchtime on Friday using the fire escape when partners are lurking

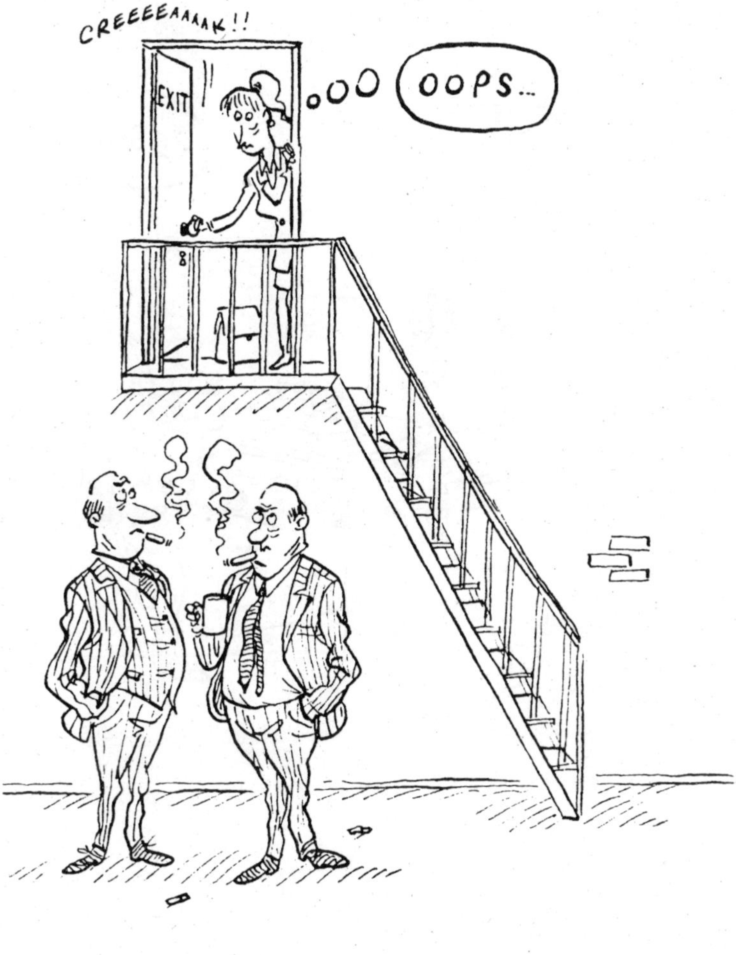

Use up the senior partner's stash of hard drugs

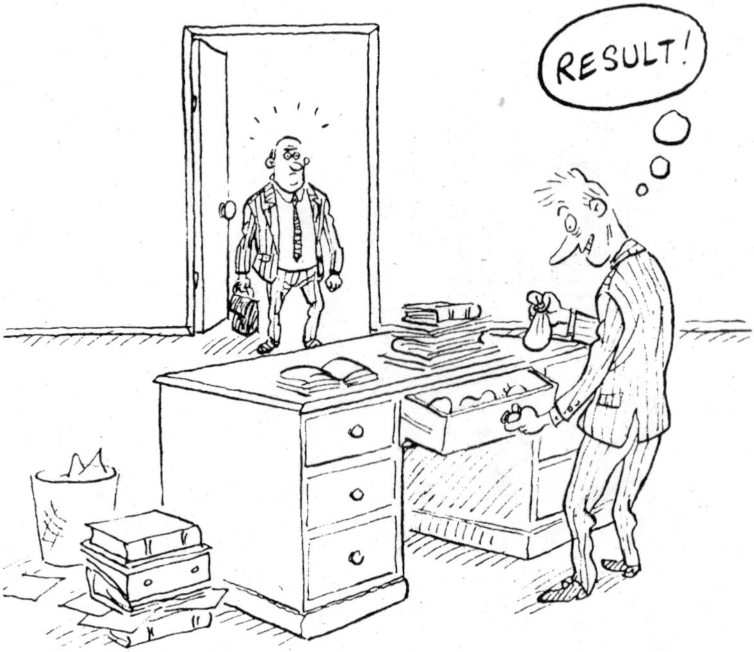

Express a robust view of international law to the US Military

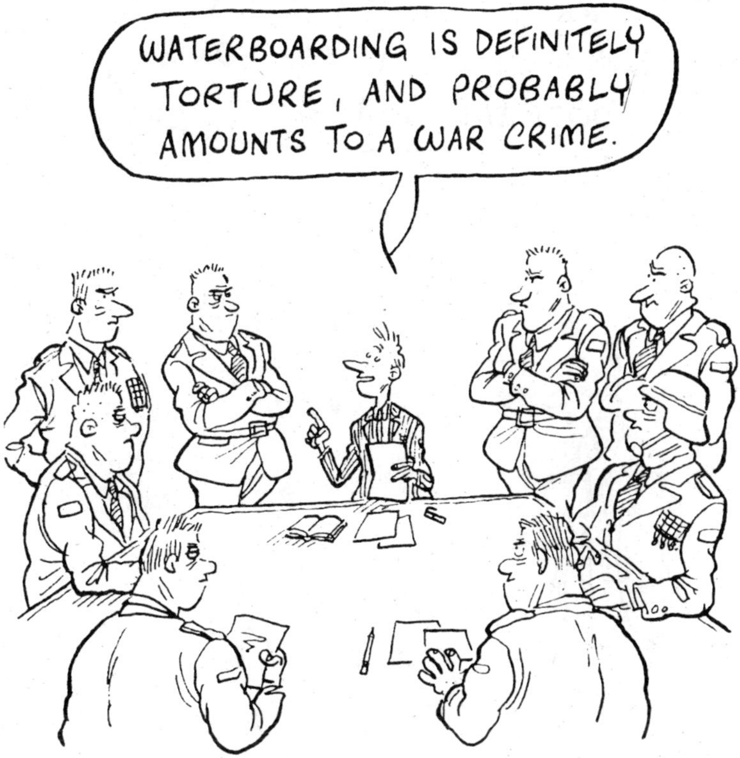

Maintain a healthy work/life balance

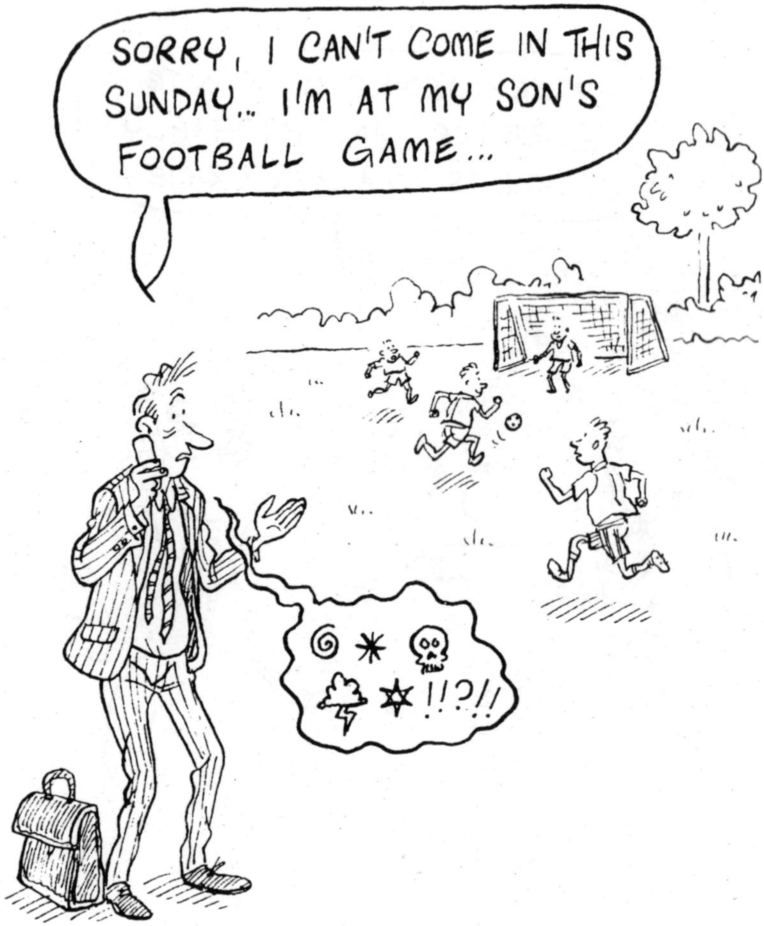

Suggest that everyone in the firm should be paid according to the hours they actually bill, including the partners

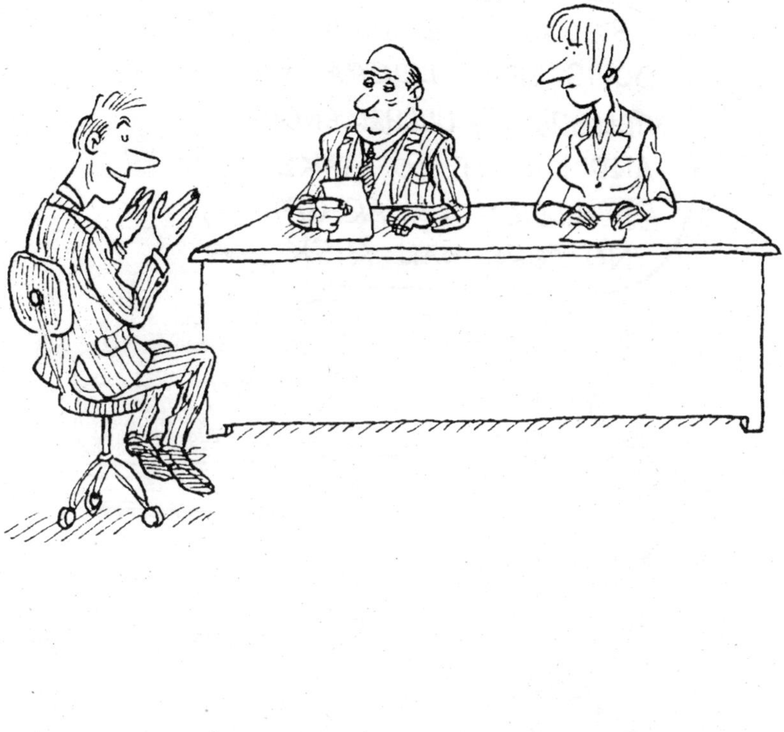

Be honest at your interview

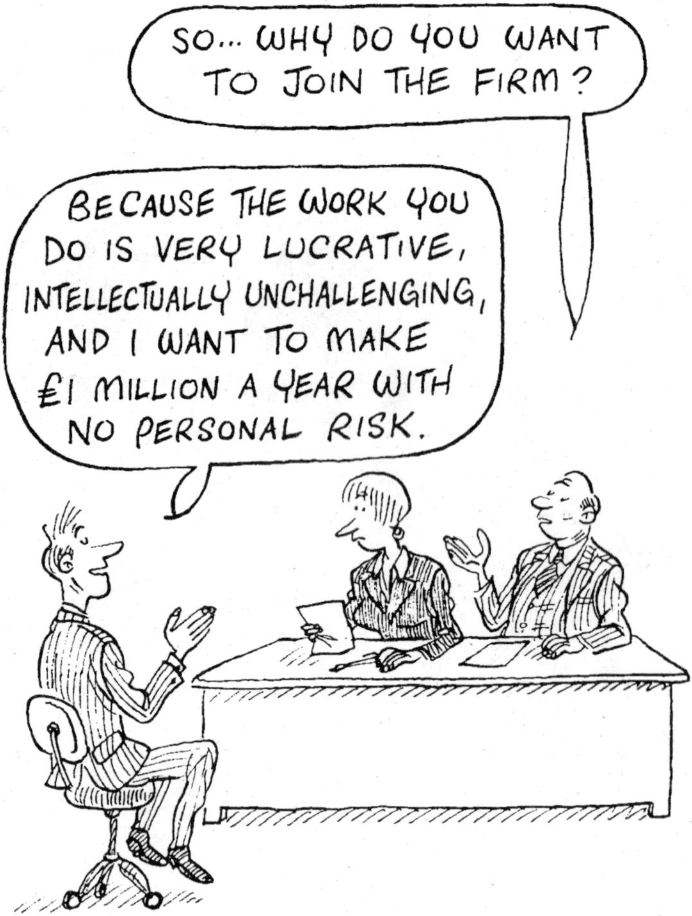

Get yourself an in-house job, then call your old firm to explain why you won't be sending them any work

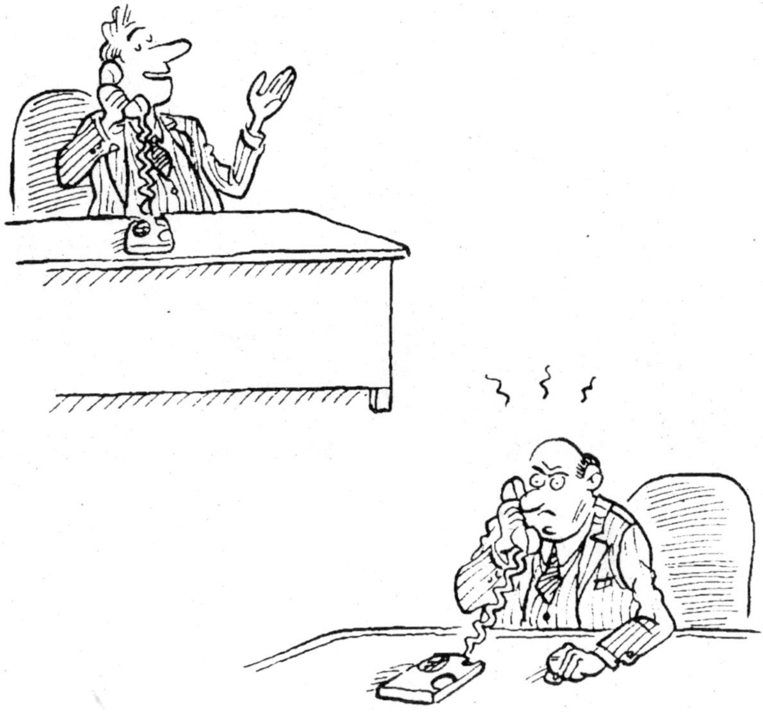

Tell the senior partner how much the partnership resembles John Grisham's *The Firm*

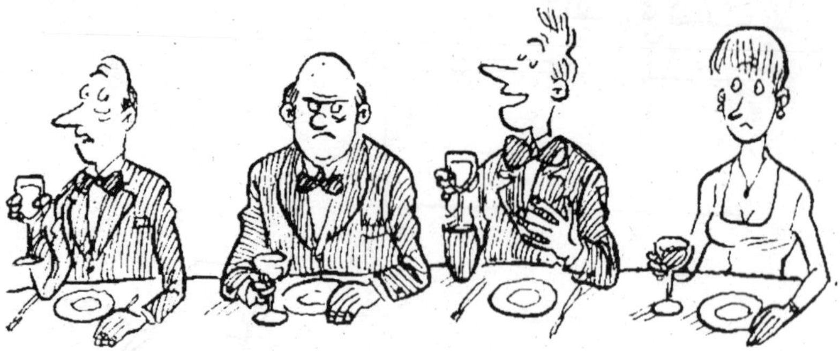

File the urgent business you're not qualified to deal with in a locked cabinet

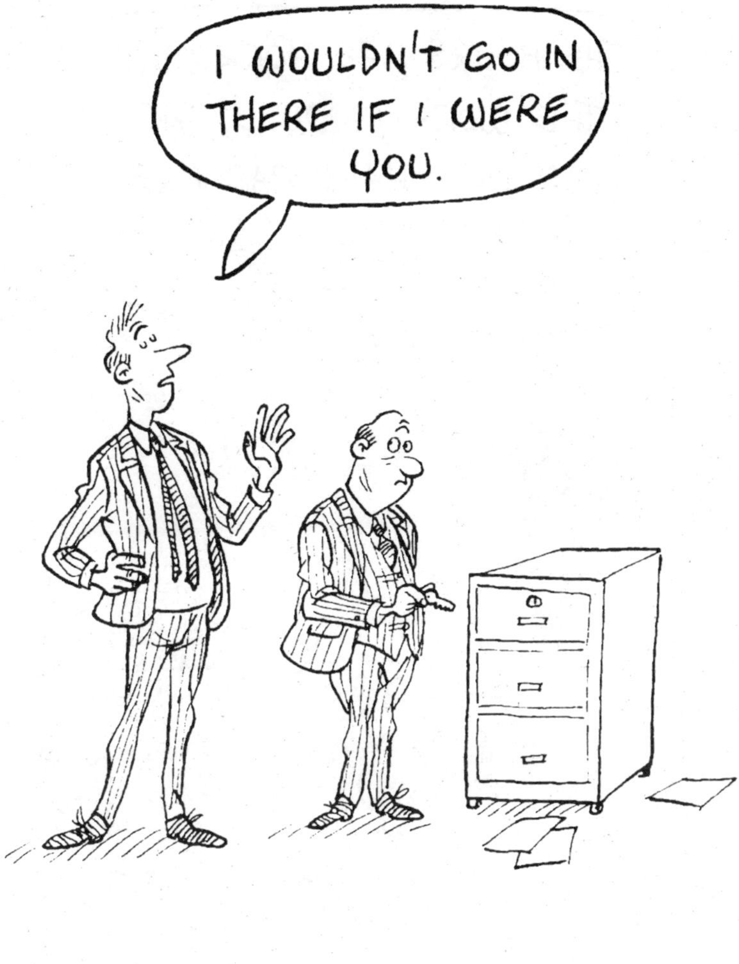

Go back to your old school and give the Leavers' Day address

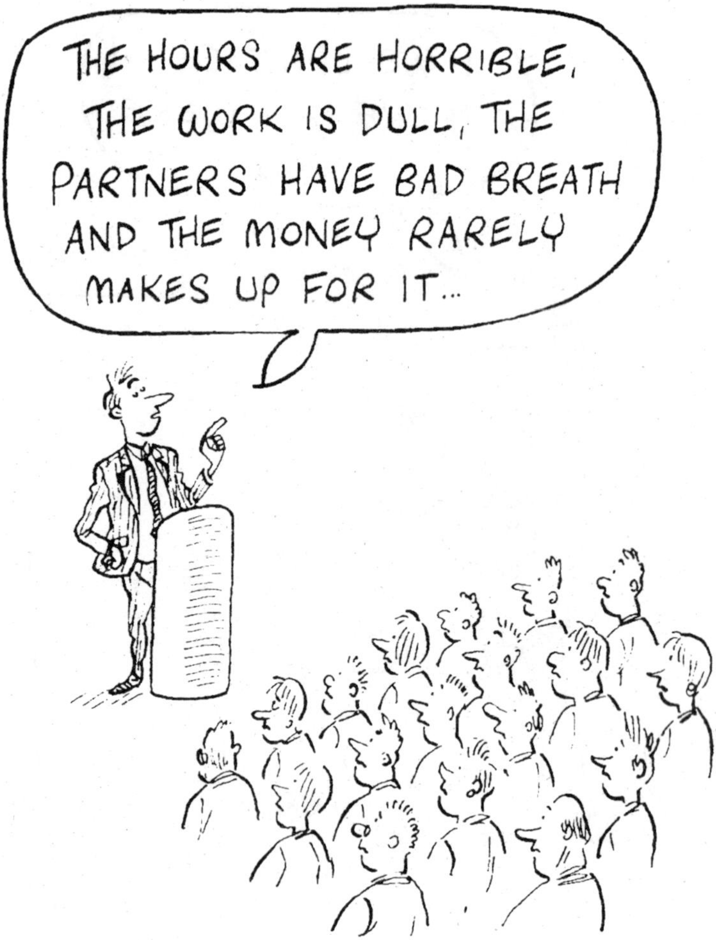

Pose as Playmate of the Month

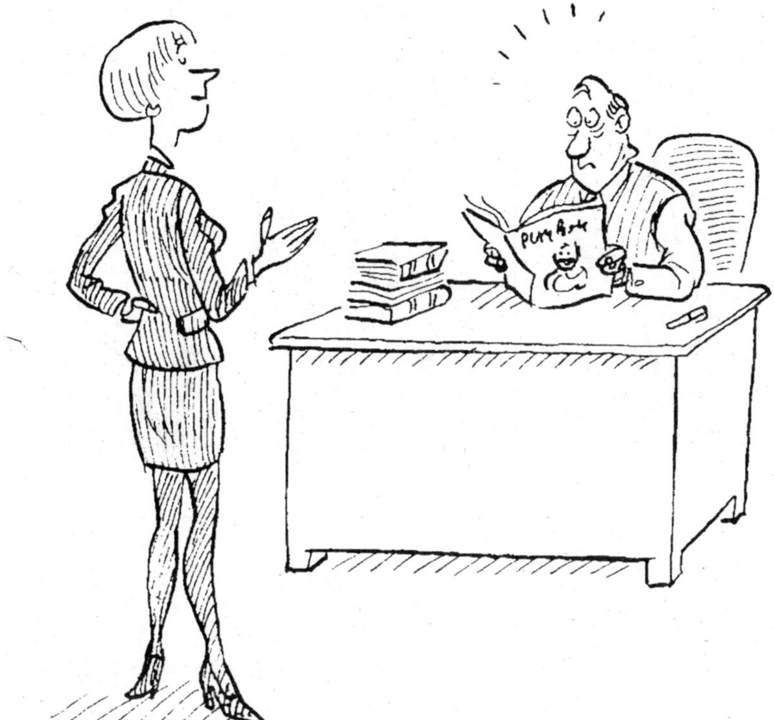

Make jokes about 'those losers in IT', forgetting that they know all about your internet use and can have you fired for it

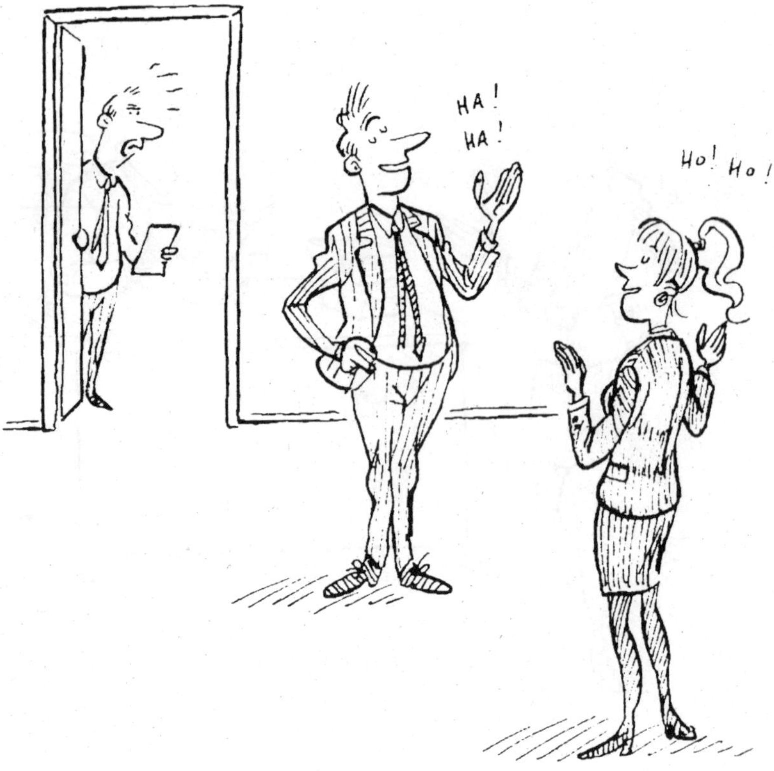

Explain at your interview at a huge commercial litigation firm that you want to be a lawyer so you can help people

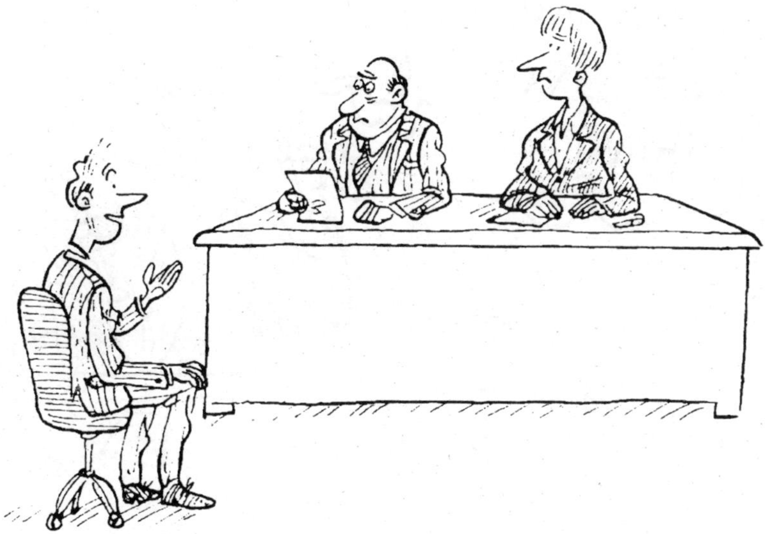

Dictate your correspondence after a long liquid lunch

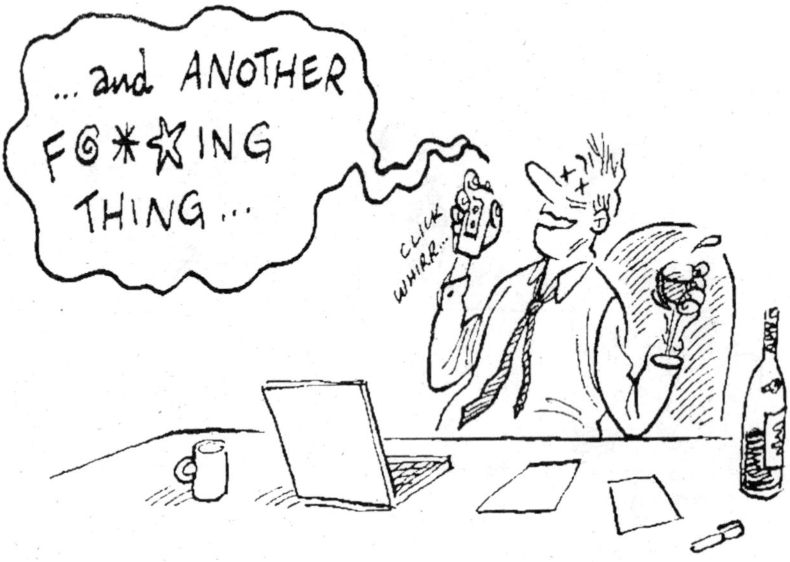

Explain to your client how, by the end of his case, there will likely be no money left as he will have spent it all on legal fees

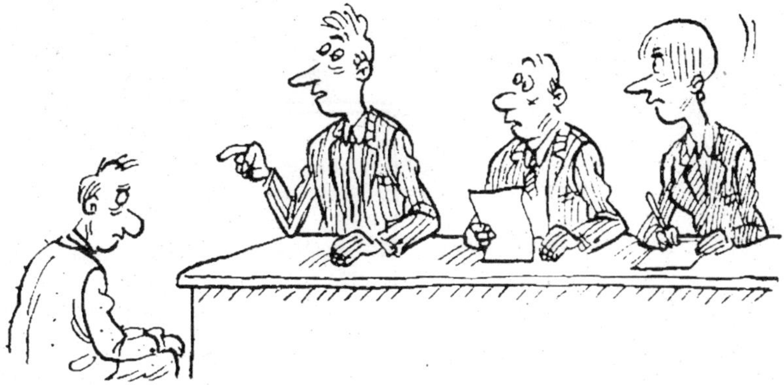

Moon the judge

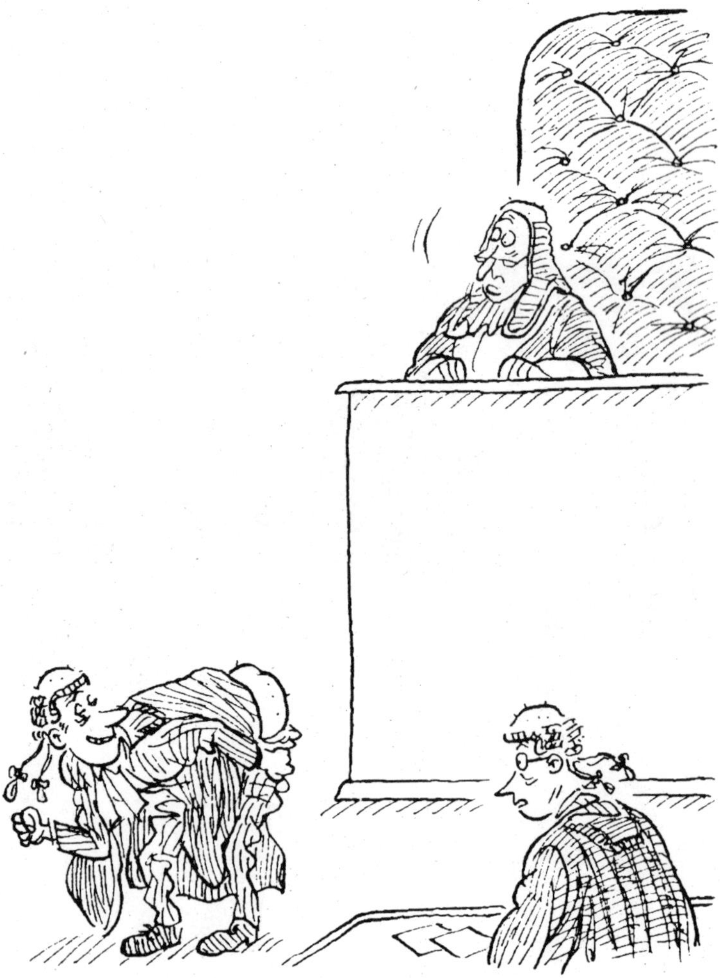

Be honest at your annual appraisal

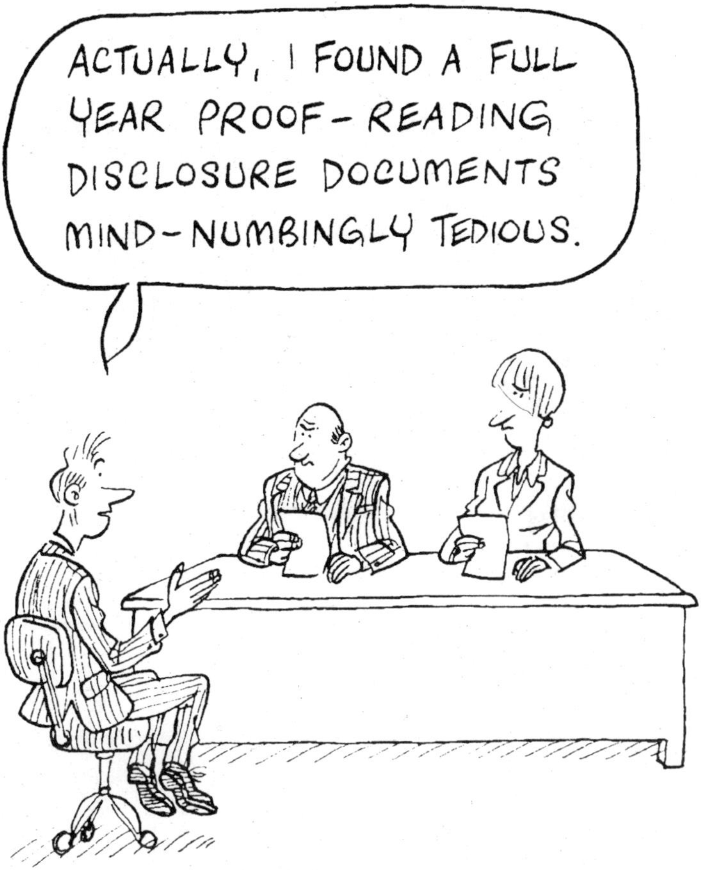

Tell your client how his fees *really* get spent

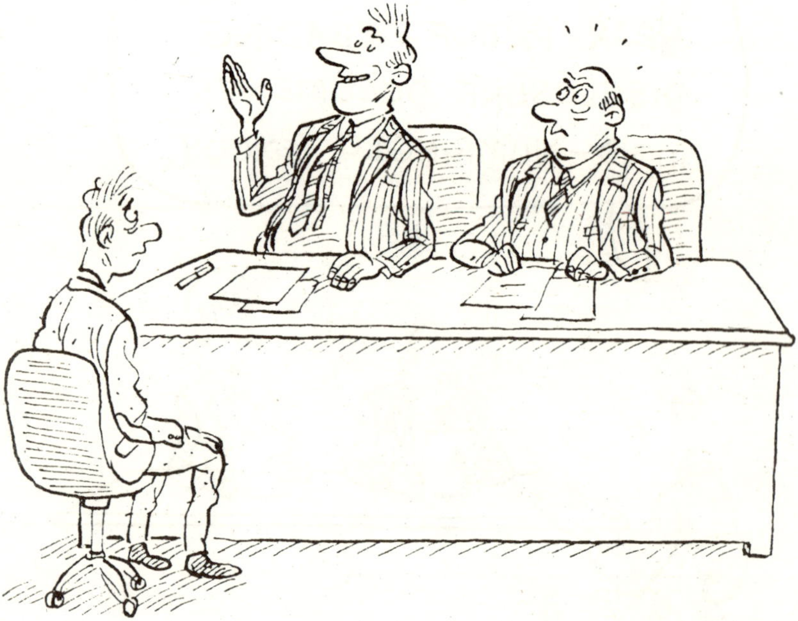

Bare everything in the Big Brother house

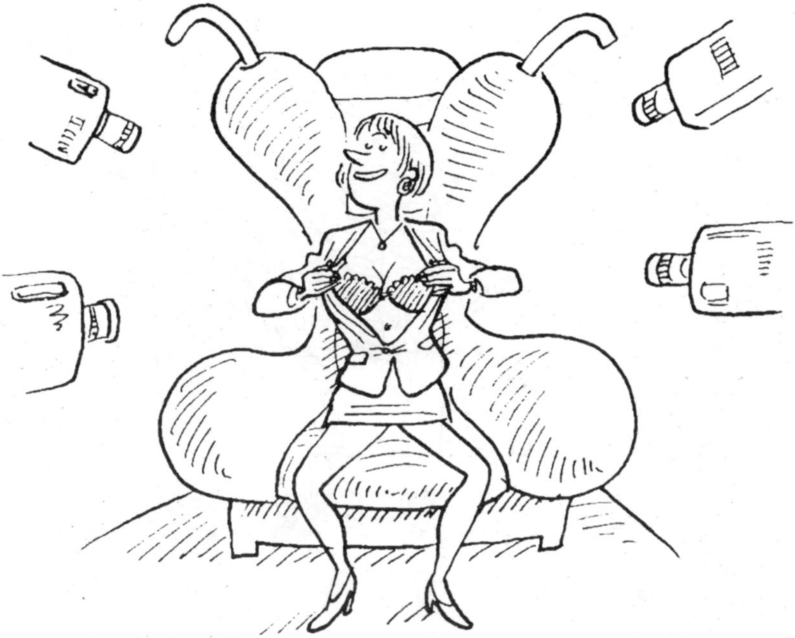

Celebrate Bonfire Night at the office, in style

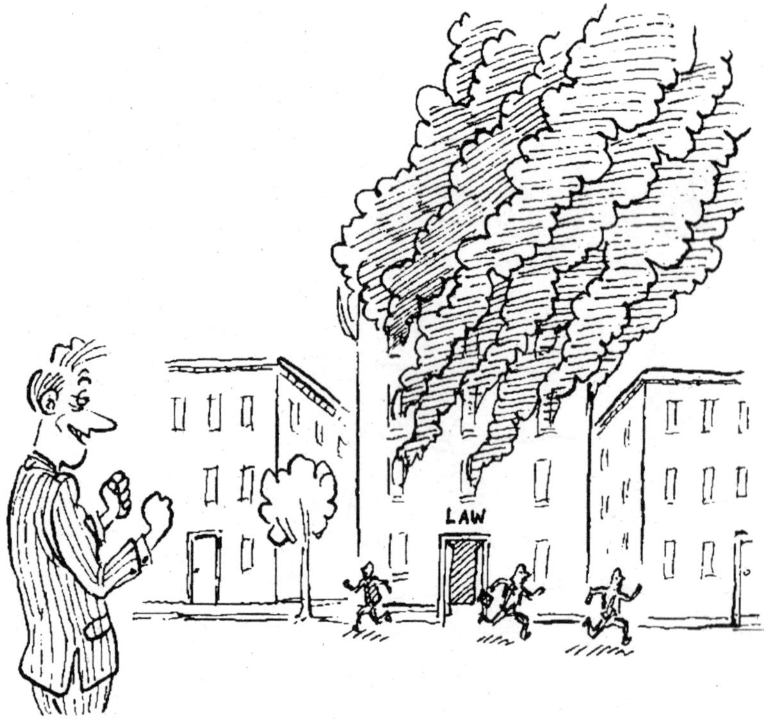

Demonstrate your skills as a mimic just as the senior partner walks past

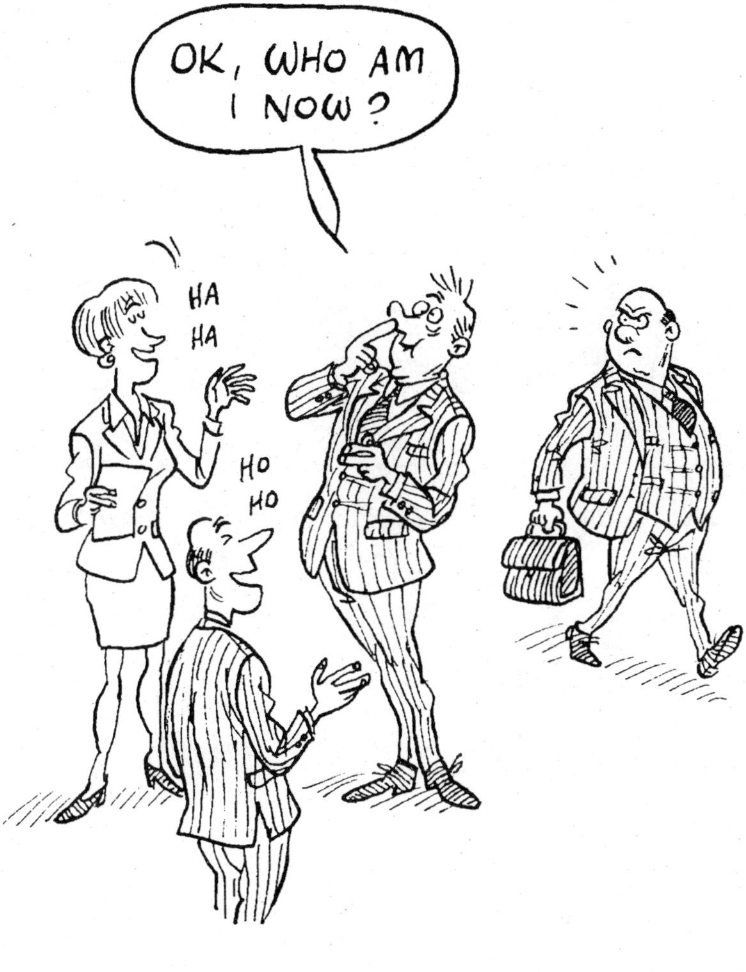

Ride your Harley Davidson around the office

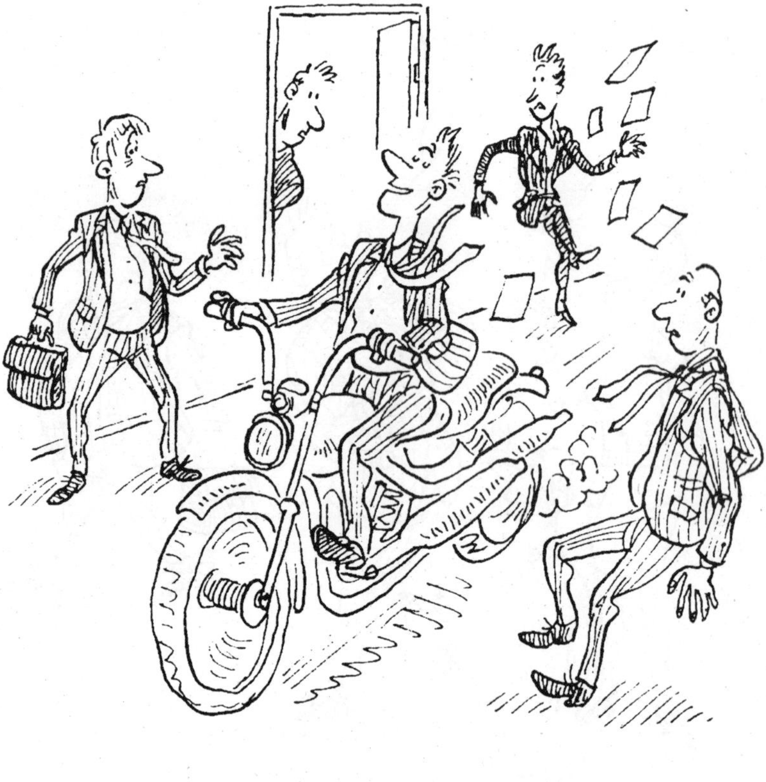

Explain to your client that your firm didn't lose the case because 'you got the wrong judge', but because the firm was negligent, and he should sue for damages

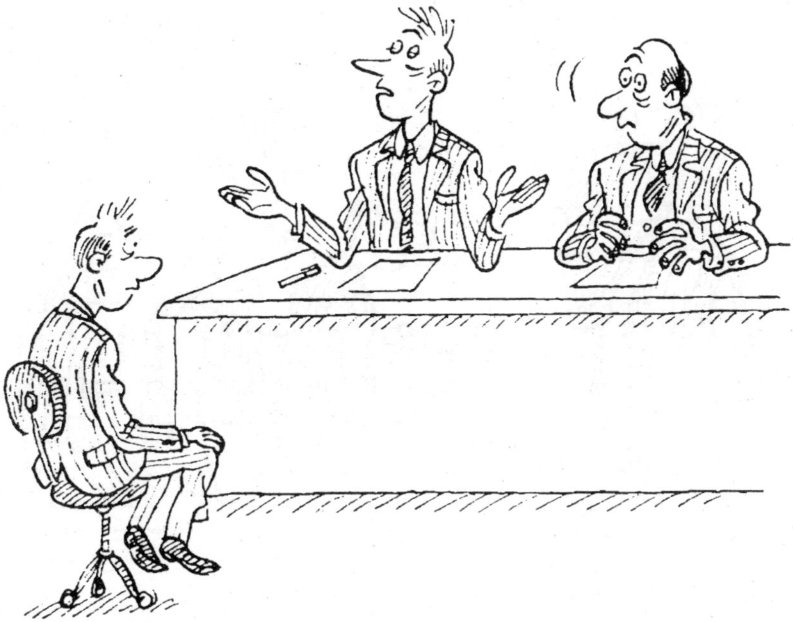

Tell the senior partner that you turned down a £10 million account with Philip Morris due to ethical concerns

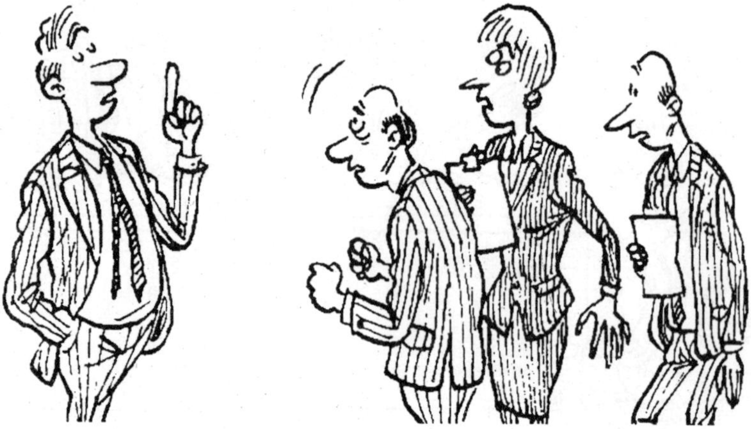

Host your next client conference in the nude

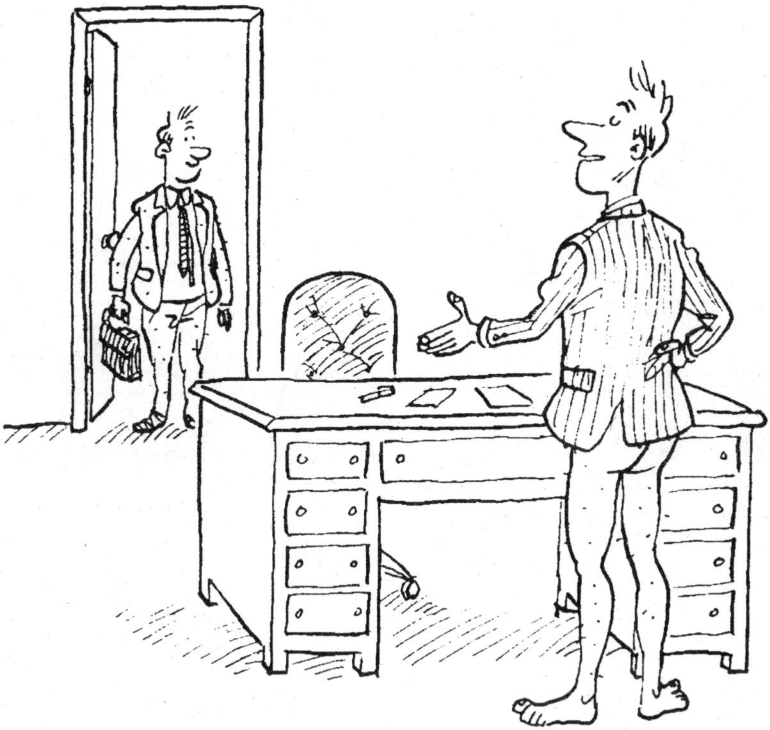

Telephone the Inland Revenue and give them full details of the partnership's 'business trip' to Antigua

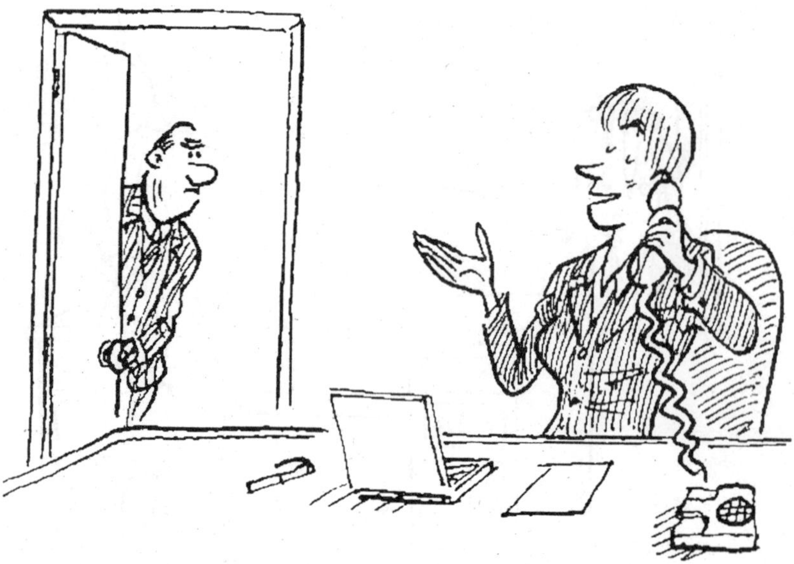

Explain to the senior partner's wife which intern her husband has been having an affair with

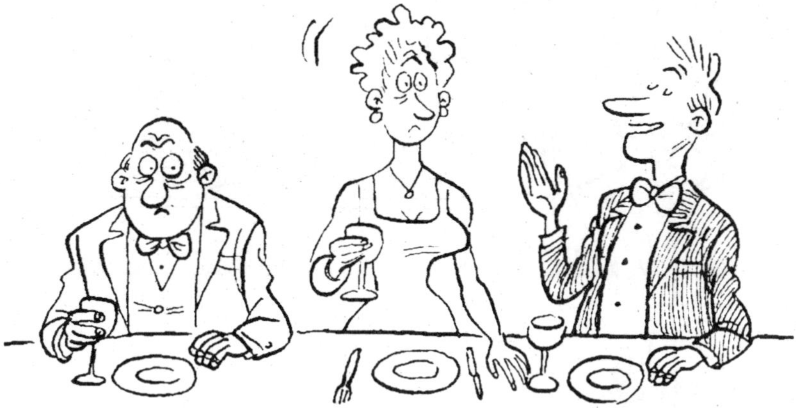

Be a capital markets lawyer, in a recession

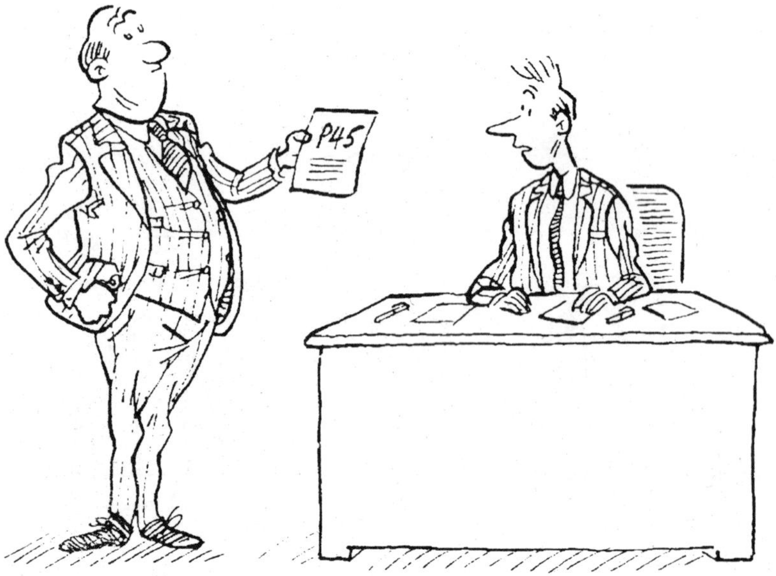

Date a page 3 girl

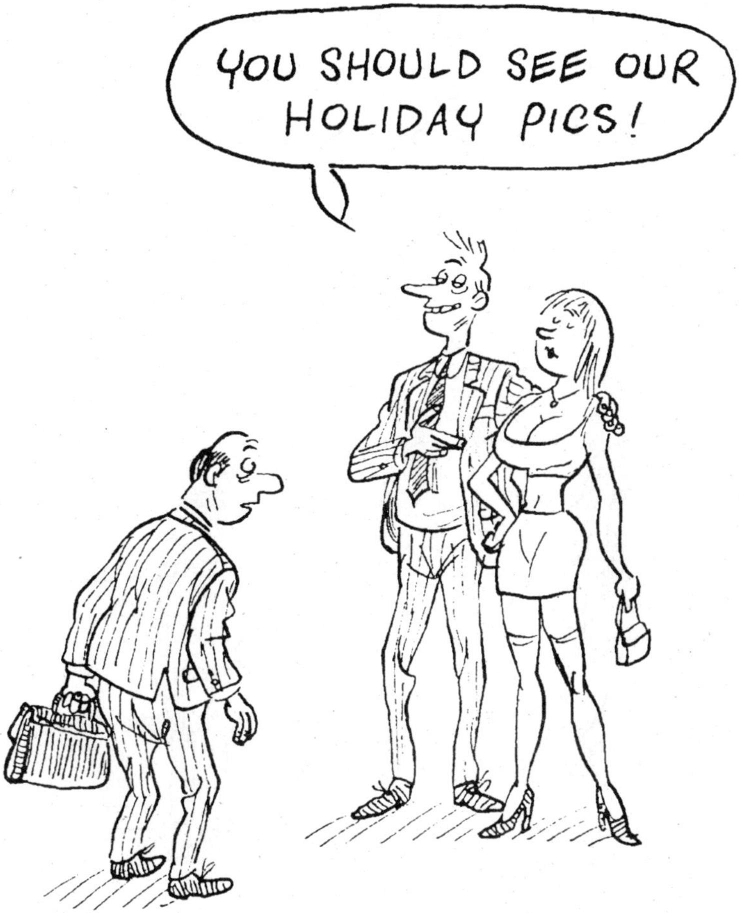

Psychoanalyse the partners

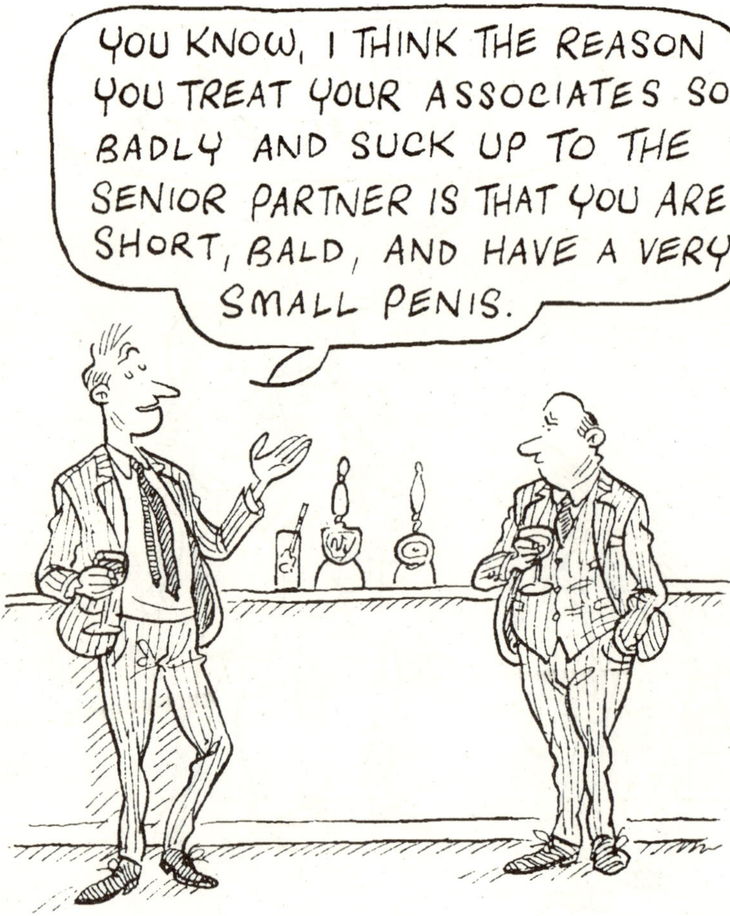

Mount the senior partner at the Christmas party

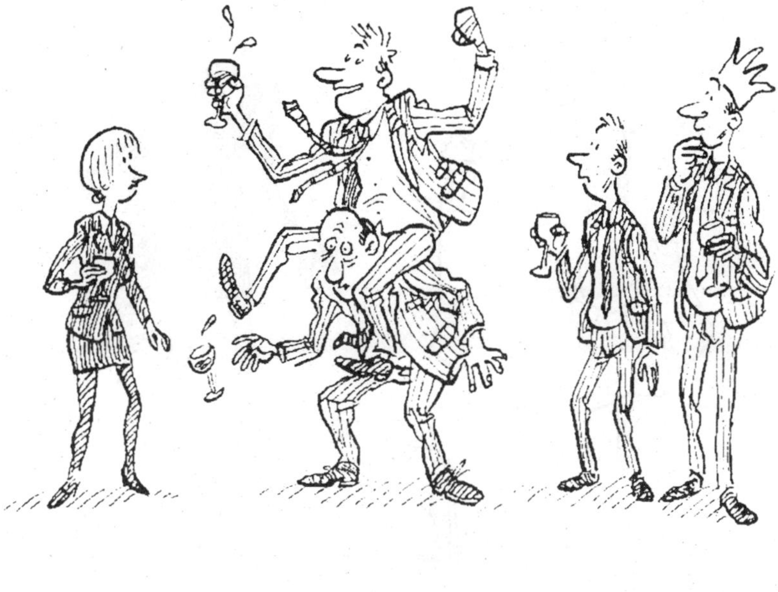

Engage in full and frank disclosure

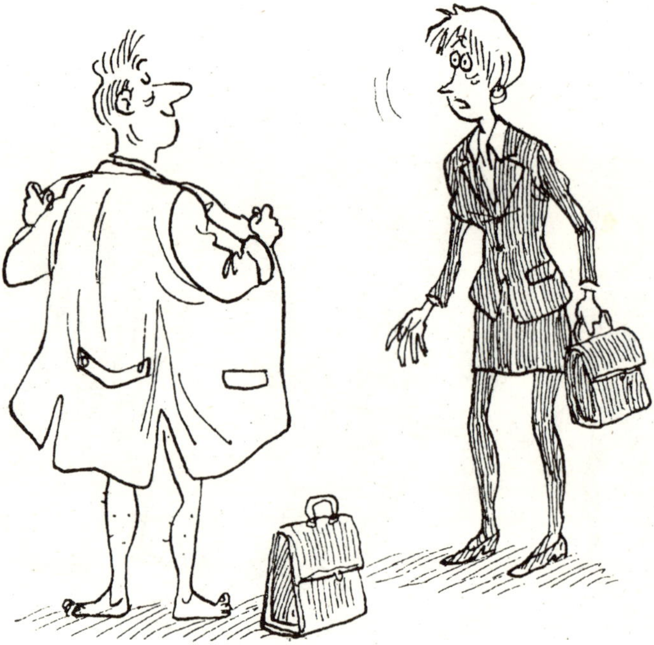

Explain how a conflict with your social life prevents you from working this weekend

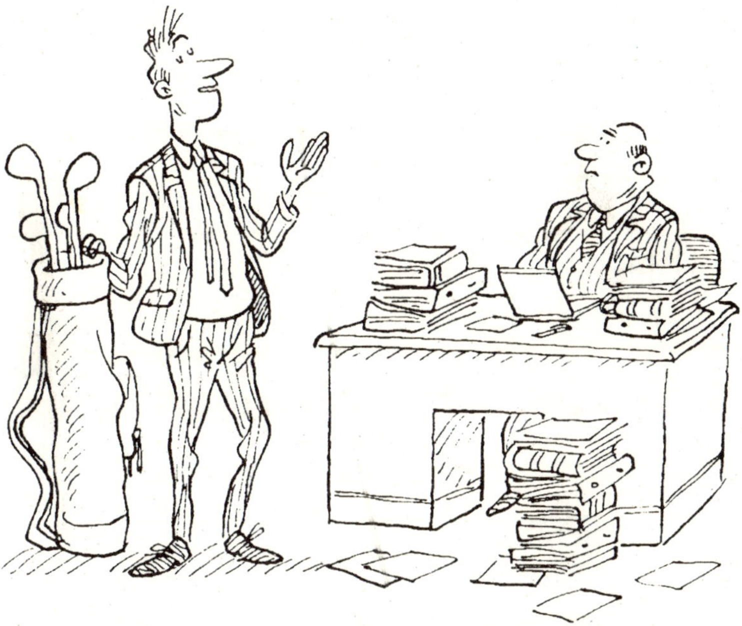

Move to the South of France and 'work from home'

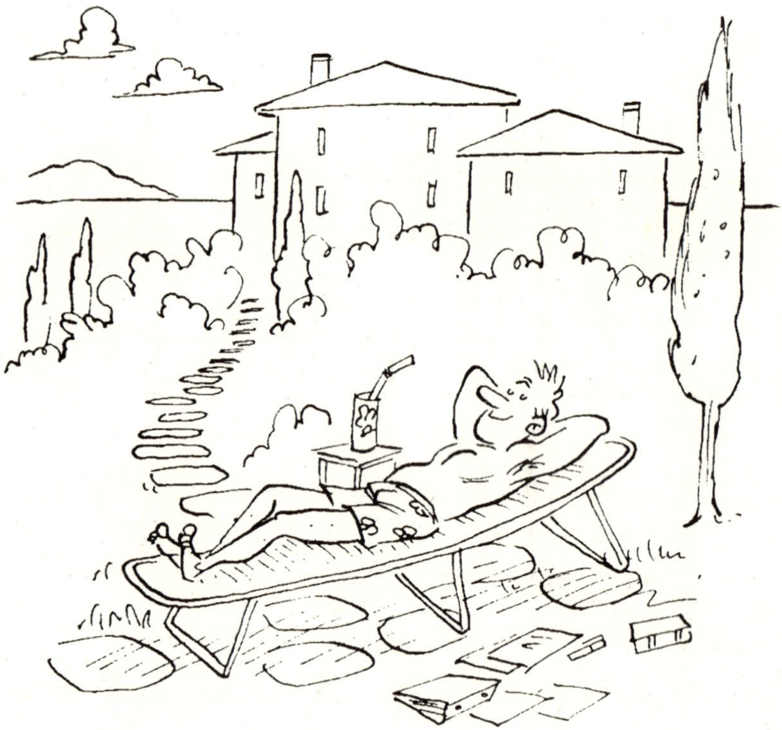

Sign, name and date your sincerest thoughts in the firm's confidential suggestion box

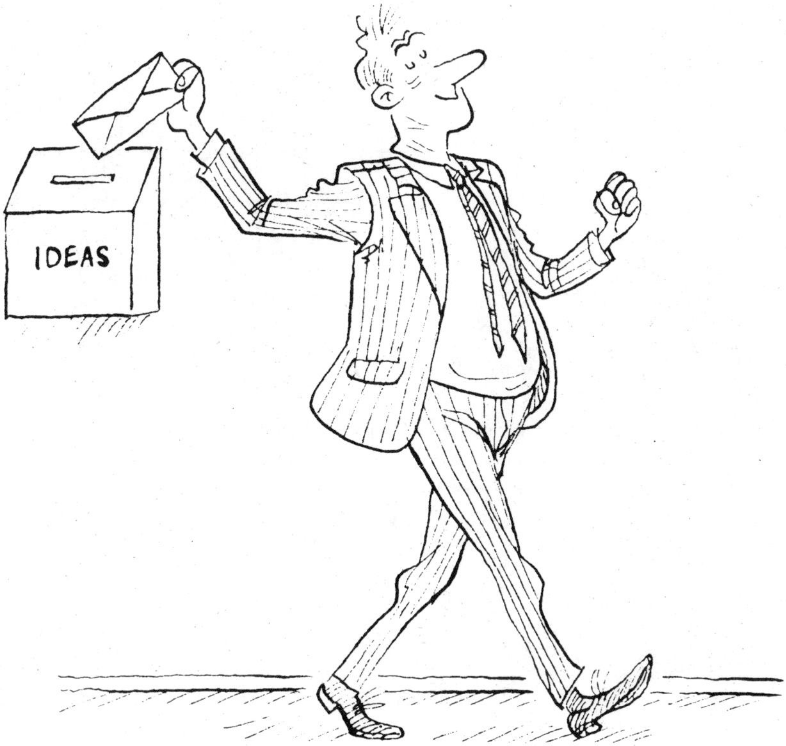

Tell the summer interns that life at the firm isn't really about free drinks and trips on the London Eye

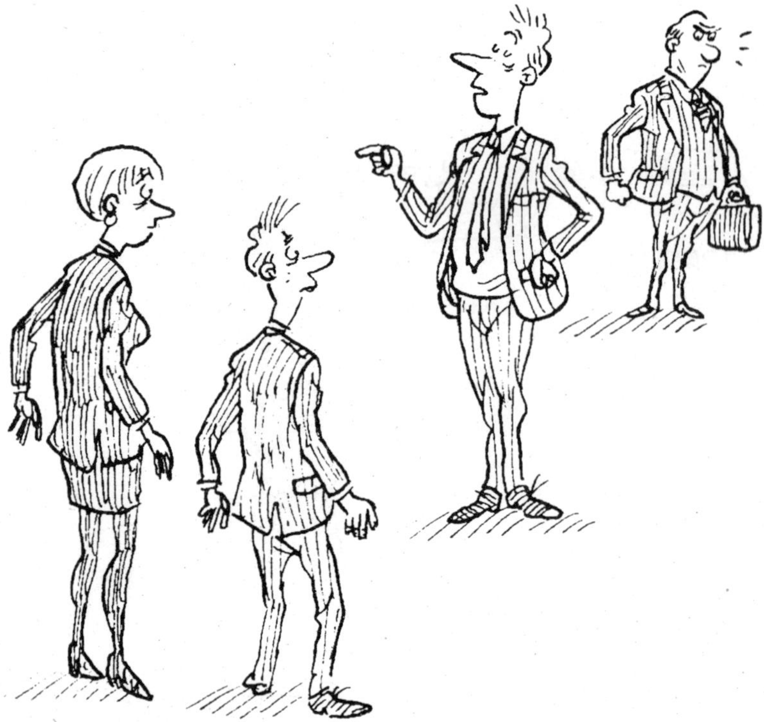

Tell the senior partner that, no, his nephew can't have a summer internship because that would obviously be nepotism and unethical

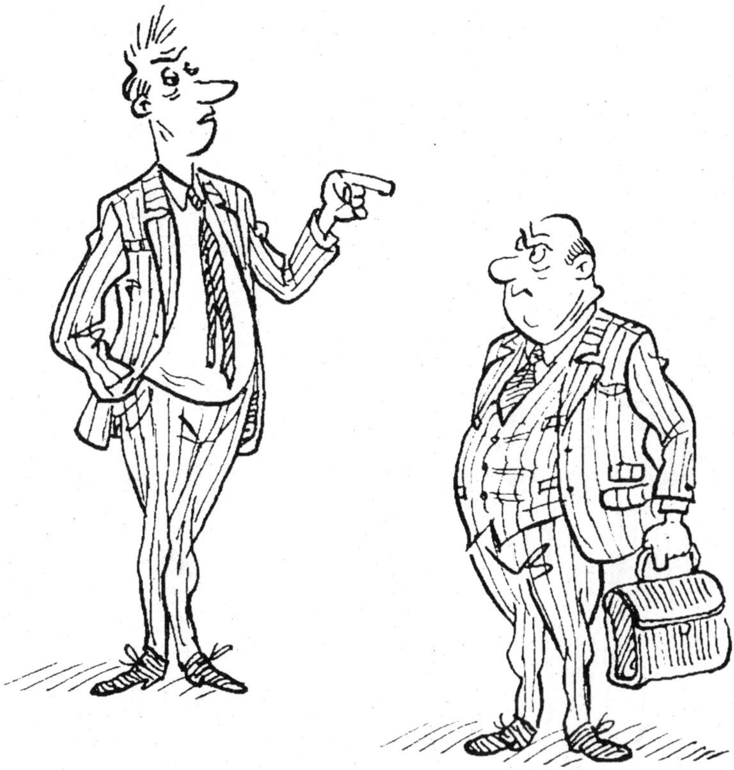

Ask the judge if you didn't by any chance meet him at a swingers' party last Saturday night?

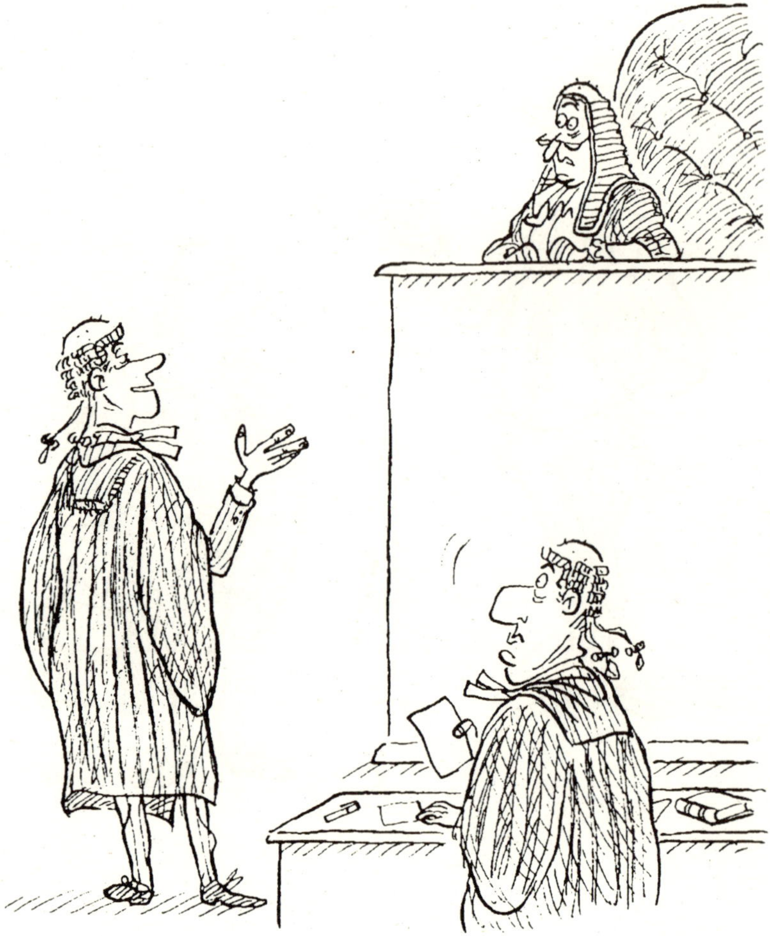

Hack into the firm's website and make it more exciting

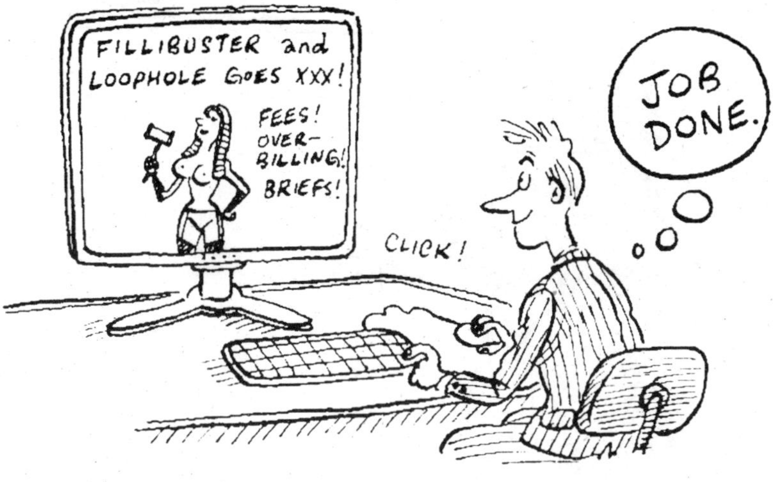

Dress as Batman in court

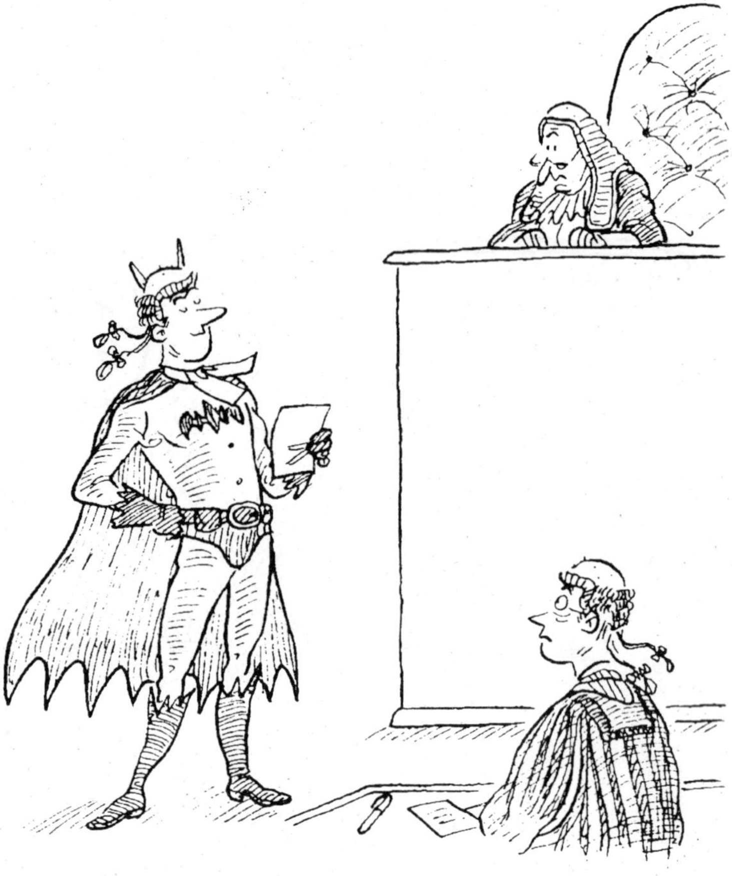

Tell the judge what you *really* thought of his ruling

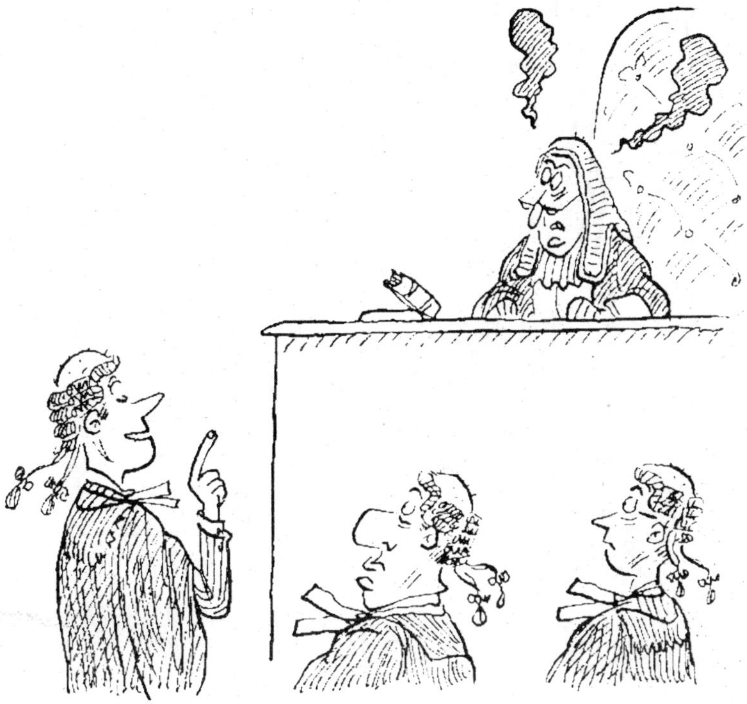

When the 99 per cent white, male, public school partnership annouces that 'diversity is our number one priority', snort with derision

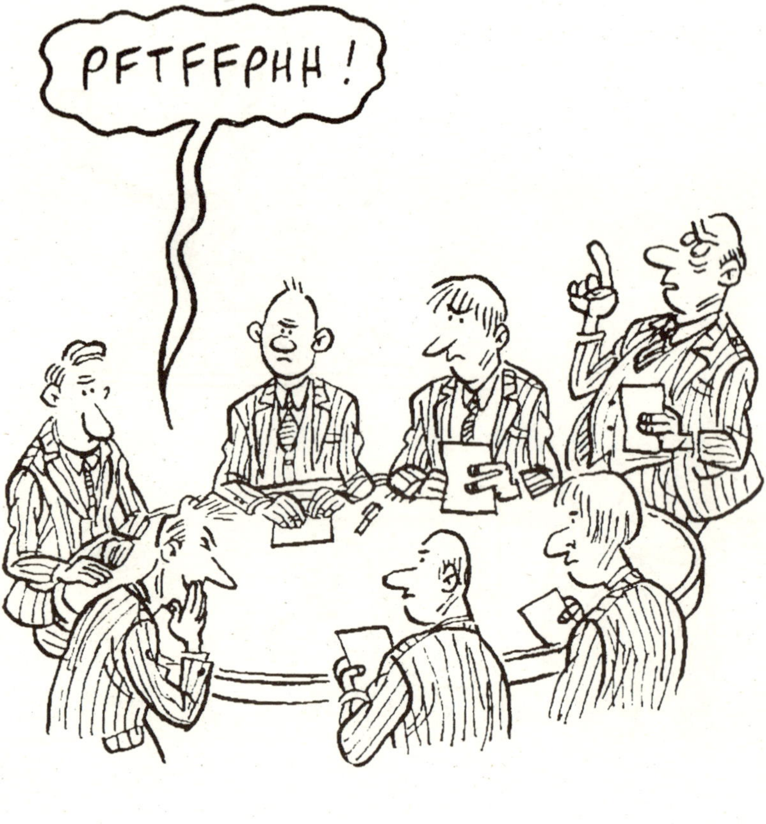

Write an email making a vicious personal attack on the senior partner . . . and then copy him in by mistake

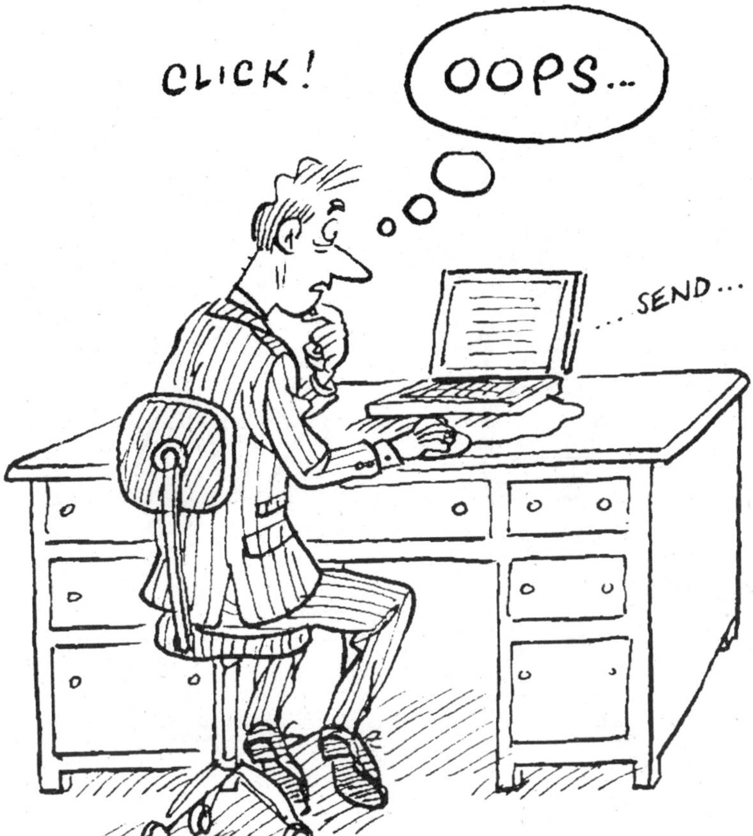

Wear a short skirt (especially if you're a man)

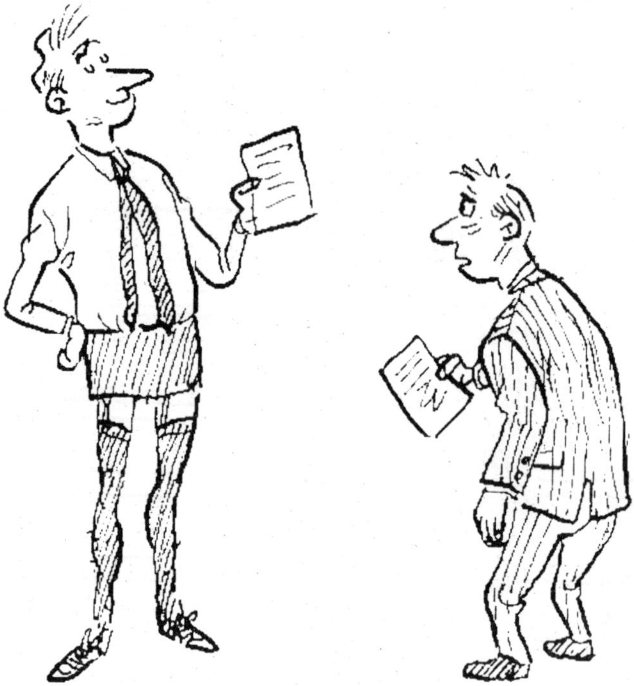

Tell the judge to 'talk to the hand'
(because the face ain't listenin')

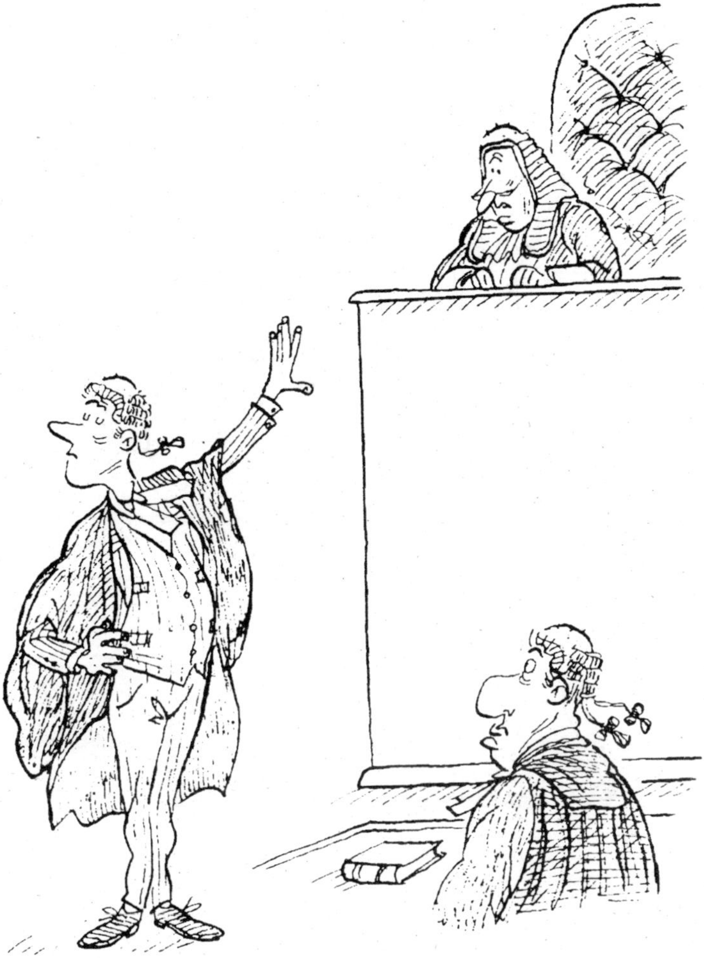

Host your stag night in the office conference room

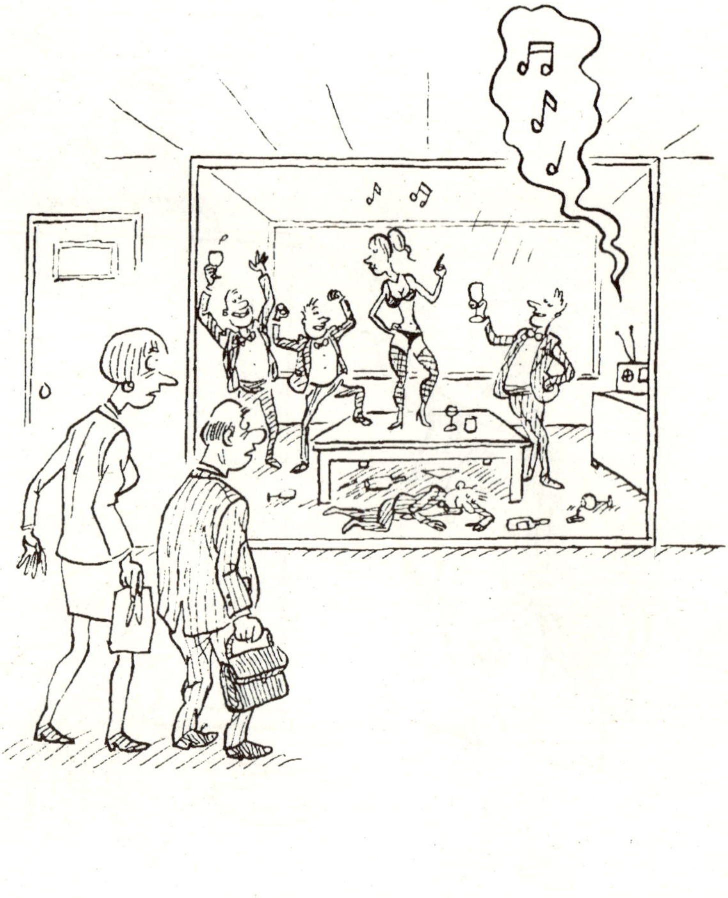

Tell the interviewees what's in store for them

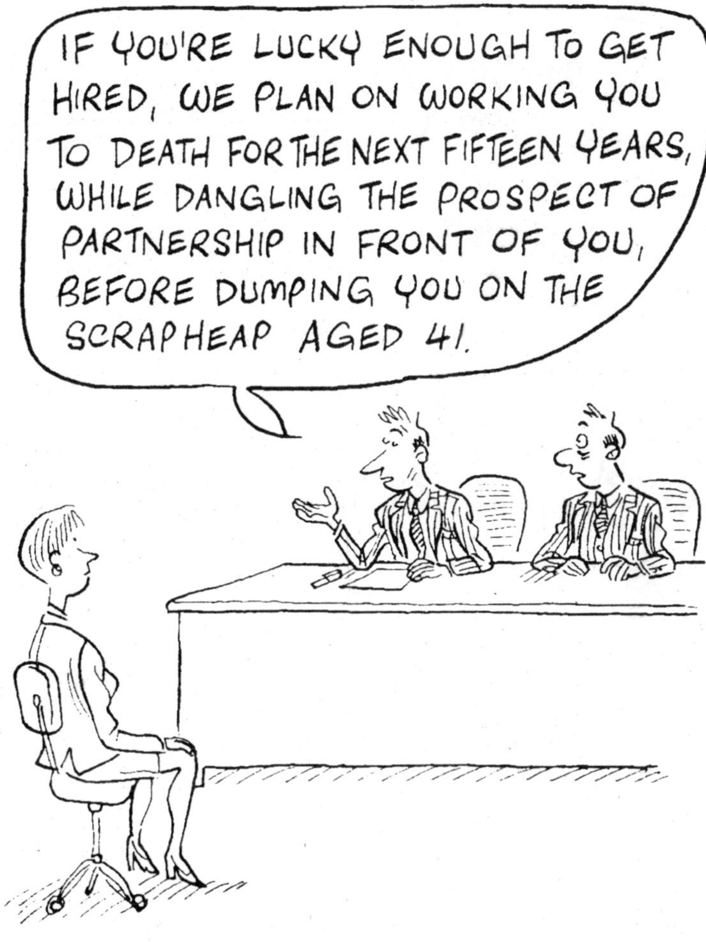

Contract an illness which can only be cured by regular bouts of surfing

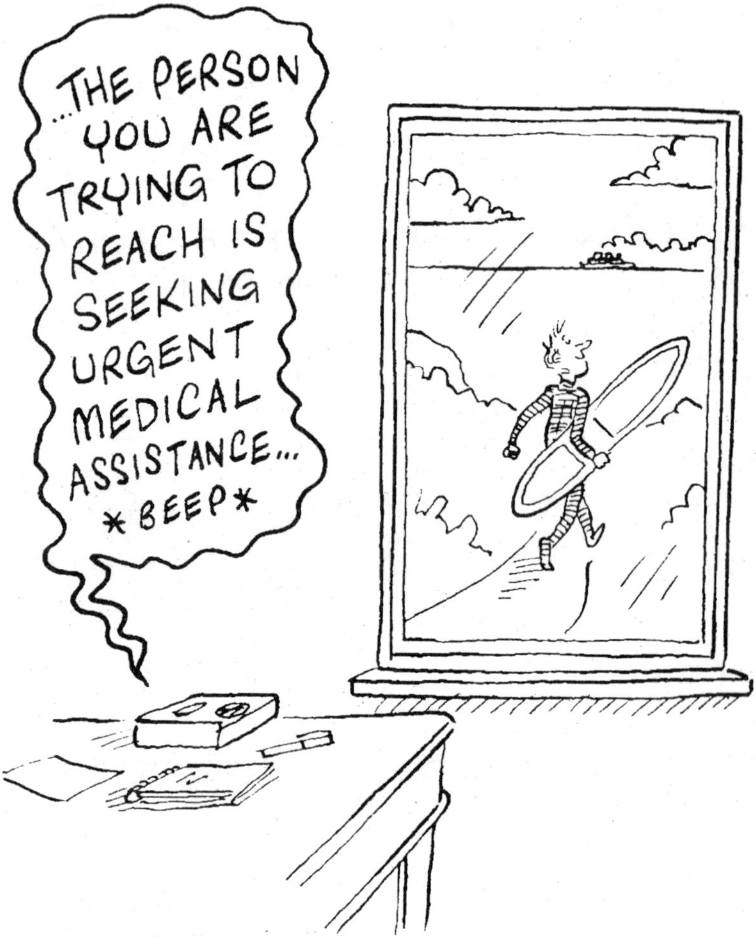

Write this book

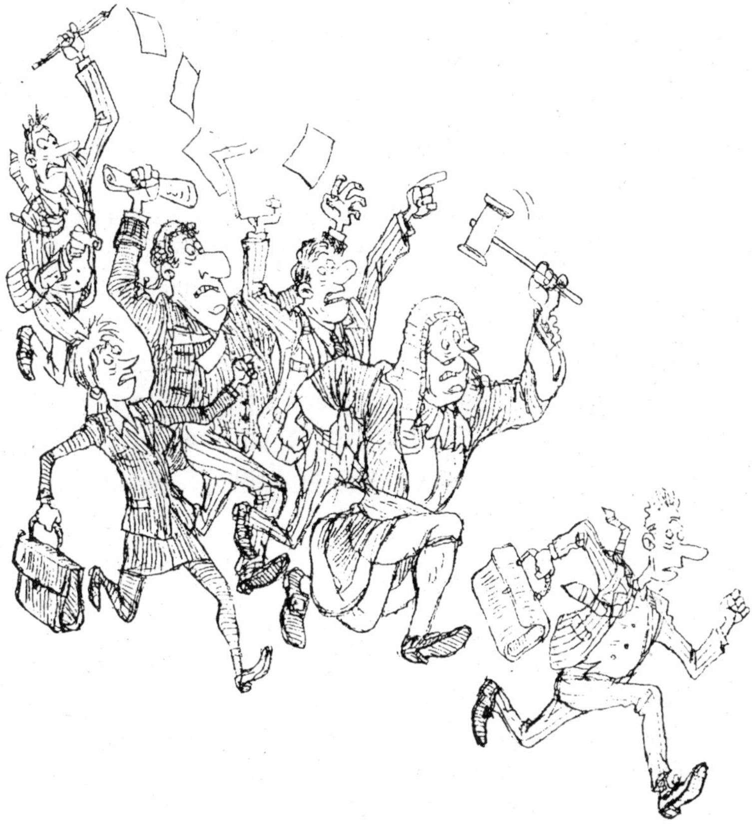

Alex Steuart Williams is a former barrister turned cartoonist and feature film animator. His movie credits include *Who Framed Roger Rabbit?*, *The Lion King*, *The Iron Giant* and *Harry Potter and the Half-Blood Prince*.

Alex is something of an expert on leaving the law – he treacherously abandoned the bar in 1996 and since then has spent a good deal of his time making fun of his former colleagues. His cartoon strip Queen's Counsel has been published in the law pages of *The Times* since 1993.

You can see examples of Queen's Counsel cartoons at www.qccartoon.com, where you can also buy original drawings and prints at absurdly reasonable prices.

Previous books by Alex Steuart Williams:

Queen's Counsel – A Libellous Look at the Law
Queen's Counsel 2 – Judgment Day
Queen's Counsel – Laying Down the Law
The Best of Queen's Counsel
Lawyers Uncovered – Everything You Always Wanted to Know But Didn't Want to Pay £500 an Hour to Find Out